WHISKEY'S CHILDREN

WHISKEY'S CHILDREN

JACK ERDMANN WITH LARRY KEARNEY

Kensington Books
http://www.kensingtonbooks.com

KENSINGTON BOOKS are published by

Kensington Publishing Corp.
850 Third Avenue
New York, NY 10022

ISBN 1-57566-305-8

First Kensington Hardcover Printing: October, 1997
First Kensington Trade Paperback Printing: July, 1998
10 9 8 7 6 5 4 3 2 1

Printed in the United States of America

INTRODUCTION

The book you are about to read is, for my money, the first beautifully written book on alcoholism since Frederick Exley's *A Fan's Notes*. Indeed, it is one of those rare books that is at once profound and entertaining as a movie; in the case of alcoholism and recovery, as *Lost Weekend* or *The Days of Wine and Roses*. *Whiskey's Children* is the true story of one good person's descent into a life where one feels surrounded by the grease pit of despair. The walls of alcoholism are sheer, and every time you try to climb out, you just slide back down. It is a life where the outward signs are hideous—the devastating effects on one's spouse and children and friends and career and health—and yet where the things that don't show are even harder to bear. The inside of a practicing alcoholic looks like self-loathing, agony, insanity, attempts to start over, failures, rationalization, suicidal exhaustion. And it feels like a small miracle that Mr. Erdmann, working with Larry Kearney, has, with both horror and grace, captured the crazy mosaic of it all.

Alcoholism surely affects someone in your family. It is an

addiction where the body tells the mind that it must have this substance to live, this substance that will then destroy and degrade both the user and those around him. It is an addiction typified by use, bad consequence followed by further use, and worse consequence followed by further use, and disastrous consequence followed by further use.

It is a living, bewildering nightmare.

A recovering alcoholic I know, a doctor now sober 20 years, captures the pattern of alcoholism when he describe's 3 phases: the first phase is fun, the second fun and trouble, the third is trouble. Erdmann and Kearney paint all three stages with bold stroke and brilliant nuance, even sometimes with devastating humor. *Whiskey's Children* begins in an alcoholic household in St. Louis in the year 1934, where Erdmann, the son of a noted jazz pianist and a chorus girl, first became aware of his father's drinking, and of the destruction it wrought. "I don't want anyone to think that this is the story of a child abused by a family—it isn't—it is the story of a family abused by alcohol," he writes. And his own abuse of the drug—the fun stage—began when he was 13 and discovered that a little port would fix him, would kill the pain. The fun lasted almost ten years, then moved along into the fun and trouble stage where for 15 years alcohol seemed to work for him. Of course there were problems—a marriage built on alcoholic dependency that ended in violence, a descent into mediocrity in a once promising career, his deeply wounded children. And this was the fun and trouble stage.

This trouble stage reads like one of the rings of Dante's *Inferno*. The emotional battering of his children whom he loved so deeply left him inconsolable, but there was always alcohol to kill the pain. Alcohol came first; the addiction always came first. His life became one of despair, insanity, jails, institutionalization and worst of all, the most intense loneliness and fear one can imagine. Hallucinations, paranoia, suicidal longings, lock-ups, it's all recounted here with total honesty, an absolutely compelling narrative drive, and even lyricism. This story—a glimpse into the soul of a highly intelligent and very funny family man, a brilliant salesman who also happens to be a pathetic alcoholic, is so beautifully told that it will leave you shaking your head with wonder. Even as this person careens toward certain death, one finds oneself mesmerized by the hugeness of the drama, rendered in perfectly captured detail. God is in the details, they say, and so is the destruction.

But then a miracle happens. Against all odds, the insanity stops.

The Epilogue chronicles something that happens for all too few practicing alcoholics, which is arrival on the path of absolute abstinence, of rehabilitation, and even redemption. Recovery, as experienced by Mr. Erdmann, meant reincarnation—the chance to build a new life out of extraordinary pain, a new life that was sane and fulfilling and abundant. This all began for him in yet another dry-out house, where at the very end of his rope, sick and drunk and dying, he heard another drunk read the words, that "God could and would if He were sought." And Erdmann knew in that instant that he didn't have to hurt anymore.

It was a long period of detox and restoration, and the discovery that the chemotherapy he needs to stay alive is a spiritual way of life—not religious, but spiritual. In rooms full of other recovering alcoholics, he was shown the steps of recovery—the surrender, the internal cleansing, the cleaning up of the wreckage of the past. He was taught to get out of himself and to become a person for others. He was taught some twenty years ago how to rejoin the human race.

He writes about the way he lives now, the life of unselfishness and kindness and empathy and honesty that is necessary for alcoholics who never want to drink again, one day at a time. He lives a life without alcohol or other mood-altering drugs, and not only participates in life, but thrives, making a daily difference to countless other alcoholics. I am one of those people whose lives were saved by meeting him, by him sharing his experience and strength and hope with me 11 years ago. When I met him, through a friend, I embodied a description from this book: "If you're an alcoholic, and you live long enough, this is where you're going. It's a place. It's a goddamned empty train station where it's cold and the sun is just going down." And I saw, in his life, grace made visible. It did not seem possible that this could happen for me, but he reached out his hand as he has to so many others, and brought me into that grace. I never knew him drunk, but through a weaving together of these pages and my own shabby, scarred years of drinking, I now do. I know him sober too, and this is a great man to know. You would be hard pressed to discover a more vital and wise and honorable man. I am grateful beyond words to have met him when I did, and I am thrilled for people who don't know him and can now look forward to meeting him in *Whiskey's Children*.

Hang on—you are in for the ride of your life.

Anne Lamott

ONE

I'm four or five years old and my mother and sister are out and I'm still half-dressed in the dim light of the living room. The venetian blinds are pretty much shut, and there are lines of sunlight fuzzed on the slats.

There isn't anything to do. I could go outside but I don't feel like getting dressed. There's a radio but I'm not allowed to touch the radio. It's very large and wooden with stretched fabric and arched mahogany paneling. There are tiny rooms and tiny people in it, with silver microphones.

I'm waiting, really, for my mother to come home. Dad just got up and I can hear him moving around upstairs. I'm standing near the piano but I don't touch it. Anywhere you are in the living room you're near the piano. Over it is a dim, floral still-life, rose and peach. If you look through the slatted blinds, the outside is a lovely, blurred green from the lawn. The lawn is the place to look for four-leaf clovers.

The question right now is how he's going to be when he comes downstairs. He's a big man with a strong, dark head, and he fills the narrow staircase. When I think of him now he's lit from behind, with clear, sharp edges.

Thinking about him, I see him standing in the street, waiting for us in his dark suit and beige raincoat. His hands are in his pockets and he's rocked a little back on his heels, with his hips slightly out. The perfect image of cocksure, his clothes fit as well as his polished, black hair. Cold eyes with a secret grievance and his mouth a little soft and a lot contemptuous.

I guess we remember parents in characteristic poses, but this is very strong. It seems to me that most of my father's attitudes were struck. In my upturned eyes he had a graven, oversized, electric clarity.

My mother is small and delicate, with big, Colleen Moore eyes. She's Irish and Catholic, and prides herself on the legs of a professional dancer. She very much likes to show them.

She fights with my father instinctively and well.

My sister Pat, is lovely, quiet, and just outside the maelstrom. She's three years older than I am, and Dad wouldn't dream of hitting her. At any rate, she never gives him reason.

I sit quietly in the living room. I wish I could turn on the radio.

I wish I could turn on the radio and I wish Mom would come home.

Dad is coming down the stairs. I see his slippers first. His left slipper is his weapon.

He has on his black suit pants and one of those shoulder-strapped, ribbed-cotton undershirts.

I go behind the table in the dining room and wait, quietly. He looks awful, with his hair and eyes tangled and bleary.

He doesn't see me and turns down the hall toward the bathroom. "Goddamn," he says to no one.

I come out and around the table slowly. It's big, heavy and polished. In deep shadow it fills three-quarters of the dining room. It doesn't leave much room in there and since he's a big man, the dining room is where I run to get away. I can move fast, through and around the table legs. He can't.

I open the front door quietly and sit down on the steps. All the front windows have curved-end awnings, green-white-orange. The lawn slopes a little to the sidewalk. It's quiet.

I'm holding the soles of my feet in my hands. My back is curved and my head up, like a plaster-gnome bookend.

I didn't close the door behind me all the way, and I can hear the water running in the tub. I hear him come out of the bathroom and move down the hall. He turns on the radio and something like *Thou Swell* comes out, with a jumpy, cut rhythm.

I haven't started to wish he were dead yet. Even when it finally comes to that it's a last-ditch thought at the dead center of a thousand wishes and alternate worlds where things are changed just enough to let us be the Maybeck family down the street. To be like the Maybeck family with its easy familiarities, the kids with an easy sense of their parents coming off them like the light off a glossy illustration in an expensive children's book.

I don't want him to die yet. I just want him to smile at me. I want, too, to be proud of him; to have him do things just to make me proud.

For a Saturday, the street is very quiet.

Mom and Pat are downtown and I'm chewing a blade of grass from the side of the steps. There's a morning breeze blowing and my pajama top is thin. I'm getting cold, so I slip back in and plunk in the big armchair. We're not supposed to sit in Dad's chair. It's not a hard rule, it's just understood. I can hear him in the kitchen at the ice-box. He slams the door and comes down the hall.

The break between the dining room and the living room

is a stucco, almost moorish arch. Standing there he fills it
up. His towel is over his shoulder and his hair is slicked back.

"What the hell are *you* doing. Put on your goddamn slippers. Where's your mother?"

"She went downtown with Pat."

"Goddamn. George sucks hind tit again, just like always.
Get your goddamn clothes on."

He heads back down the hall to the bathroom just as the
footsteps start up the path.

Mom comes in with a big department store box. Pat is
carrying a brown grocery bag. Mom looks around and turns
down the radio. She's put the box on the piano bench. She
works off the lid and there's a great mass of fur inside.

"Isn't it wonderful, Jack?"

It comes straight up out of the box when she lifts it, dark,
soft and heavy.

"It's muskrat, Jack. Isn't it wonderful?"

She swings it on her shoulders and twirls once so it flares.
Her feet are light and they trip out a little presentation dance
step.

"Why aren't you dressed? Run upstairs and get your
clothes."

Her left hand is rubbing the coat against her thigh. I know
now that for a woman who seemed to have a minimal interest
in sex, she made a lot of overtly sexual gestures. Sometimes
they embarrassed me. She raised her skirts too high.

Pat hasn't said anything, she just takes her bag to the
kitchen. On the way up the stairs I hear the back screen door
thwack as Pat leaves, charmed as ever.

When I'm dressed I come down and peer through the
blinds to see if any of the kids are out. It's still quiet. Mom
is running water in the kitchen. The bathroom door is right
off of the kitchen. I hear it open.

"Where the hell have you been?"

"I had to go downtown to get my coat."

"What coat?"

"This one."

A little coquettish and "I told you so" airy. She's probably doing her twirl on the linoleum.

"And where the hell did this one come from?"

"I bought it."

"The hell you did. Where did you get the coat?"

I've started to move in a sleepwalk with slow, turning steps. I put one finger on the piano bench like I'm testing for dust. There's *never* dust on the piano bench. I look at it carefully.

"I bought it on time."

"Yeah. And what did you use for money?"

"I saved it."

"Who gave you the coat?"

Dad's voice is loud. It's usually loud but now it's ragged and painful. It hurts my ears.

"Who've you been whoring around with for fur coats?"

"You son-of-a-bitch."

I've moved to the radio and I have my index finger pressed on the speaker fabric where the pulse is strongest.

"I break my ass to keep us going and you're out whoring around for goddamn fur coats. I work the whole goddamn night and what I get is no goddamn breakfast and you god-damn dancing around in a son-of-a-bitch fur coat."

Now I'm scared. I don't want to go to the kitchen but I am. It seems to take a long time.

"What do you *mean,* talking to me like that. You can't do it. I put up with every goddamn thing *and* your slut band singers and now it's this. God. The hell with you. You can just go to hell!"

Mother is shrill, but not as loud.

"Goddamn whore."

This sounds final. I run out of the hall and into the kitchen. I grab Dad's leg.

"What the hell do *you* want. Get the hell off me."

He throws me off his leg with one big hand.

"You leave him alone!" It's as loud and shrill as she gets.

Dad half turns, picks up the heavy, black cast-iron skillet, and swings the flat of it backhand into her face. It makes a terrible noise and she stands there in her coat with the blood running from her nose and mouth.

He laughs and goes back into the bathroom. I stand there and she stands there as if we were opposite sides of a coin. Frozen panic.

This is the feeling from the house on Winona St. "One should fear to strike panic into the hearts of children." I read that once. I can't remember now where. When I read it the feeling came back, the choked throat and the lump that won't come up.

Winona St. is in South St. Louis, and this is 1937. The four of us live here in a nice, middle-class house in a nice neighborhood.

South St. Louis isn't very urban. Right down the street is a big, beautiful farm. We're close to Forest Park Highlands, with its band shells, arcade and rides. The farmer down the street guards his melons with shotgun and rock salt. Next to him is a strip mine where they dig the clay for the brick factory. The best part of the mine and brick factory is the little train that runs on narrow tracks. It's a joy. The tracks are just across the way from our backyard. It's got a little wood-burning engine and an engineer with a cap. Plumes of white smoke trail from the engine. We have gas lamps too, and in the evening the lamplighter comes by, turns their spigots on and lights them up in the trees like Japanese lanterns.

The summer night air was full of fireflies. The tradesmen

made their rounds in horse-drawn wagons. "Ragman, rag-man, bottles and rags." "Strawberries, red and ripe. Straw-berries." We had an organ grinder with a monkey. I have a picture of me sitting on our lawn with it. The monkey is leaning toward my chest and my smile seems real if tentative. I remember how strange his little hands were.

My earliest memory is chasing a man who must have been my father. I'm trying to keep up and move fast through a field of mortar, empty nail boxes and jagged lengths of wood. I can't keep up and it makes me angry. I cross the narrow railroad tracks behind an unfinished house as my father goes in through a side door. Inside I can hear him yelling. I find my way down to the basement.

Surges of unexpected gladness. I spent all my time patch-ing and mending my conviction that someday everything was going to be *all right*. Sometimes, I'd open up like a breeze had passed through my ears—it happened a lot with the music. Dad played a marvelous jazz piano. That's what he did for a living. He had his own group, the Royal Palm Orchestra. Pee Wee Russell was in the band, and Dad had played with Beiderbecke and Teagarden.

I have a photograph of Russell as a young man. He's in profile, and he looks frail. The inscription says, "To George, the best pal a fellow ever had and a dark Negro piano player."

In St. Louis, in the Thirties, if you took a piece of your basement and paneled it in knotty pine, you called it a Raths-keller. That's what my father did. It was a place for him to play with his friends. He'd get a big galvanized bucket, a wash tub, really, and fill it with ice and bottles of beer. He'd set up a card table by the washroom with two bottles of whiskey on it. They'd play, and when they broke they'd surge to the liquor. Long drags of whiskey and beer chasers. Musi-cians drank. Dad told me a story once about Beiderbecke being so drunk on stage he pissed on himself. They'd play and drink for hours while I sat hidden and listened.

I'd get really happy. I'd be sitting by myself and the music would wash over me with a peculiar brightness that took me over like my head was an opening flower. Comfort, joy and all possibilities made real.

My father's music.

The fact is that except for his involvement with music, my father was cold as ice.

Colder.

He was an alcoholic, and later a barbiturate addict. With the shift from the one to the other came the slow movement from a handsome leanness to the immobile hugeness of a period sofa. I watched from my little cell as he made his visible in flesh. Fatter and fatter, and softer and softer.

The piano in the living room was a massive, obsessively tuned monolith.

He'd practice Chopin for hours, and I'd lie on the floor and listen. Carpet patterns were embossed on the side of my face. He didn't talk and he never explained. When he did start to talk it was too late. His mind was drifting, and scared.

Our hierarchy was simple and clear. Dad, the Grand Piano, Mom, Pat and me.

Across from the piano was a fake electric fireplace. The flames were revolving reflectors and beneath the fake logs was a glassy mass of fake embers. I remember the fireplace as clearly as I remember the piano.

Dad, the Piano and the fake fire.

I really don't want to judge him. There's no profit in it and if I did I'd violate the kid in my head. I have a good emotional memory and I know how I felt then. I felt all the confused love of a kid for a parent who won't, or can't, return it. I handled it as kids do. I figured the problem was me.

I have plenty of photographs from the time, but none of them are crucial. You don't take pictures of bloody fights in the kitchen. Some, though, do have a lopsided power, and when I look at them, emotions fan out in my chest like an opening umbrella.

In one I'm sitting on a pony. I'm dressed in a cowboy suit and I remember exactly how I felt. I remember the timing, too, and I know that my mother's mouth and nose were probably bruised and sore.

I don't hurt physically but I feel sad, ridiculous, apprehensive and hysterically defiant. The guy who took the picture came through the neighborhood with the pony and the suit. He had a small, thin moustache. He convinced my mother she had to have a picture of me in a cowboy suit on a tired pony. The guy must have been good.

I don't want to be on the pony. I don't want to be in the suit and I don't want to be told to smile. This feels like a turning point—like the world has started to gang up.

With all the unacknowledged sadness, I guess, of the parent who wants to believe in her child's childhood, my mother had put me up there. She was pretending about how things were. Children know about that.

The photograph is in front of me on my desk. It's in an oval frame. Feelings can't kill. When you're alone though, and the images are growing up around you like a dead city, it seems possible they could.

TWO

When she first saw my father she was dancing in Garavelli's nightclub. She saw his white, spot-lit hands. The lights would fade to black, and then a single spot would pick up a pair of bright, white-gloved hands at the keyboard. Silence for a couple of beats and a flourish swoop to a chord.

She tells me about this and when she does she flourishes her hands with a much grander, more orchestral gesture than anything you could do at a piano.

"It's completely dark now and then when the spot comes on all you can see are these beautiful white gloves" (Flora-dora-strewing gesture of the arms and hands) "and they start to play."

I love that image, and I want very much to believe in its magic. But the realness of his hands, to me, is something else again. My job is to avoid them—the way anyone avoids pain. It's typical for him to reach out and grab me unexpectedly, one big hand on my shoulder. His fingers clamp, and they have a noticeable, individual strength. I can count them.

His life is all in his hands. That's what I think. He draws

and paints and plays the guitar. When he sits practicing at the piano it's like his hands have taken him away to where everything is just the way he wants it to be.

They hang at my eye level like confused, angry animals.

Pee Wee Russell called him "a dark Negro piano player." To me that means that when Dad played he seemed to be in touch with another place, or part of him. I also take it to mean that his commitment went deep. In the Twenties something intense happened between White, midwest boys and black music. A lot of fake romantic luster has been put on it, but the virtues of the music are real enough and have nothing to do with silk stockings or bathtub gin.

Russell was an alcoholic too. It was common.

I actually heard my father express amazement at how much Beiderbecke could drink. My father wasn't one to lend another man stature, but he felt that Beiderbecke had earned it.

Music, getting laid, drinking and his mother—those were the important things in Dad's life. Sometimes the sequence changed, but that was all. He practiced every day and he womanized every day. Power, I think, was everything—receding images of pliant women opening. God knows I've shared in some of this, but never with his demonic fixity.

My mother couldn't have cared less about his dreams. Her world revolved around her children, her family and her church.

Father was George, and mother was Marian. German and Irish, with different kinds of toughness.

For me, they were natural forces, and I watched them carefully. The sweetness I felt on the odd occasion was probably just a counterweight to the futile, obsessive attention I paid my parents.

But there's still a sweetness around my memories of South St. Louis. It's not real, but it blurs the reality. The neighborhood glows in my head, and even the polished, Hollywood fakery of *Meet Me In St. Louis'* comfortable, turn-of-the-century grace speaks to me in embarrassing ways. The fact is, I wasn't born 'til 1932.

Maybe the century took longer to turn in South St. Louis. More probably the imagery is counterweight. It *is* real in my head. Solid, old-fashioned, tree-lined, airy, secret, frightening, sad and permanent—Winona St. in genteel, sunlit colors.

I know we lived other places before Winona St., but I don't much remember them. Winona St. is where I start. My sister Pat remembers them. She says we lived on Harper, near the asylum. She says Dad always joked about living in the shadow of the asylum.

She remembers we lived a while with the Bader's on Henner Street. They had a tennis court. She thinks we were there because Mom had left Dad. She knows that while we were there Mom never left her room. But I don't remember that. I remember Winona St.

On Sundays we'd leave the house on Winona to visit Dad's parents. It wasn't far. Dad would never live far from his mother. They had two shade trees in the front yard. The steps to the porch were white, and we'd go up four abreast. My grandmother would answer the door herself. I remember her hair in a strict bun, and her huge breasts. When I looked up from close-in, I couldn't see her face.

She had a stern, German face, but her body was big, round, soft and motherly. Her name was Martha.

When we were there the house always smelled of red cabbage. Red cabbage on Sunday. It sat down the hall in a pot on the spotless stove and oozed sluggish purple bubbles like a sump. I've never been fond of red cabbage, and the smell was in the fibers of the house. Probably it's common to remember grandparents' individual smells—tobacco, talcum, or fugitive brandy. What I remember is the smell of red cabbage like a bank of suffocating red drapes.

Arthur, my grandfather, was a dull man. He stood about five eleven, and he had the Erdmann jowls. The grandiose Erdmann madness, though, seemed to have passed him by. It ran straight from his father to George. Arthur lived in a rusted day coach on a spur line. It wasn't that he wasn't crazy, it was just that the craziness took a dull form. He always dressed the same on Sundays. Drab brown pants, black belt, white shirt open at the neck. He had a soft paunch.

I remember once he kissed me. I was standing by the heavy staircase in the front hall and he had one hand on the newel post. He bent down to give me a kiss. Maybe his teeth weren't in because his mouth was soft and pulpy. It was nasty. Sadly, that's my strongest memory of Arthur.

It was Arthur who eventually bought the beer-hall in Forest Park Highlands. Later he added the Arcade, and Carny grandeur entered the family imagery.

Arthur's father, Louis Karl Erdmann, was a carriage maker. Until he got out and bought the beer-hall, Arthur had worked for him painting logos and decorations on the sides of the trim, black carriages.

I have a portrait of Louis Karl. He's serious and blue-eyed in a black frock coat. On his lapel is a bronze marksmanship metal. He died of the D.T.'s at fifty-six. They were called rum-fits then, with a bit more feeling. All in all, my German blood wasn't promising.

Mom's family came from an 1831 Irish immigrant named Robert Murphy. His wife was Catherine O'Brien. Mom's mother had her own matriarchal style. Haughty and cold and full of illusory grandeur. Lace curtain.

I once opened the hall closet door in her house and there was her husband, James, sneaking a drink. He offered me one. He wasn't an alcoholic, but in that house, if you wanted a drink, the closet was the place to go.

Mom wasn't much like her mother. She was a quintessential Irish woman, though, and if her outside was flighty and emotional, her inside was a solid peasant core of purpose, order and endurance.

My father's insides were a lot more vague. I think there were drifting clots of hysteria and sentimentality in his head. He had grievances and apprehensions, and he cried the tears of the wronged. He was authoritarian but he was also a Mama's boy, and his mouth, as I said, was a little soft and a lot contemptuous. German and Irish and Irish and German, rings for her fingers and tears for her crown. They were in love.

"Well, Jack, when I met George we were both working in a night club and every night I'd take the jitney home until one night when he offered to drive me, and we were in love just like that. He was a baby. When we were married he was having an affair with one of his singers and then it was just too much and I went to my sister's and George came begging to get me back. I went back. When you're poor you can't afford a divorce and anyway, I couldn't do that. He was talented, handsome, egotistical, immature, jealous and a Mama's boy. He was jealous of my family and he was jealous of my friends. Very high strung. Later he had the nervous breakdowns. We didn't know about the drugs then. It was all right, though. I remember the last time I went with him in the ambulance and he said, 'Marian, I've always needed you, haven't I?' and that made it all right. Now I'm getting sentimental."

I hear a lot of things in her voice, but mostly the bending toughness that got her through. It stood her in good stead, and when the time came that she had to become a father too, she was up to it.

Mom began dancing professionally when she was fifteen. She had a friend named Virginia Ascher, and one day on a downtown streetcar they decided they were ready for vaudeville. They'd been taking dancing lessons together for years. They went straight from a booking agent into a job. They called themselves *The Two Jazz Janes,* but when someone told them it sounded vulgar, they became *The Kelly Sisters.*

On her own, Mom became an Ambassadorable at the Ambassador Hotel. She did four shows daily, five on the weekends—fifty dollars a week, a lot of money. When she danced at Garavelli's she met George. George's show biz was of a different order.

The clichés of the Twenties jazzman's life are clichés because they're true. All of it—bathtub gin, speakeasies and open touring cars at night with empties clanking on the floor.

"A dark Negro piano player."

Dad's Mom sent him for violin lessons. I have a picture of him at twelve or thirteen, dressed for the camera in Mozartian finery and a powdered wig. He's holding the violin like it's a stick he'd just used to kill a snake. He doesn't just look like an arrogant kid. He looks like an arrogant kid with a secret, and someone you really wouldn't want to cross.

He taught himself to play the piano. By the time I was born his orchestra had pretty much disbanded. But they'd still come to our house to play, and I remember the line of tall men with cases coming through our door.

I'm coming up the front steps between my mother and her mother. The sun is out and it's probably ten o'clock. There's a strange black car badly parked at the curb with its right front wheel on our grass. The front door is open a little, but the screen door is shut. The women are holding my hands so my arms are straight up. I can hear vomiting sounds from inside.

Two strangers are standing by the piano bench. The saxophone on it is gold. One of the men has his back to me and he's holding a tin bucket. The other is half-stooped, holding my father by the biceps to keep him from falling forward as he throws up. There's the soft, spaced, heaviness of the vomit hitting the bottom of the mostly empty pail.

I look up at my grandmother. She's already turning away. Next time it's a clarinet player holding him over the bucket. That's the way Dad was. He always got someone to stick around and help him out. He could turn the arrogance off, I guess. I think the arrogance was built around his special relationship with his mother. It was built on fine sand and he projected a secret helplessness that women, especially women, picked up on.

George and Marian hated each other's families. They'd fight about them. Especially George's sister. He worried about her in a way that wasn't quite right. Out loud. What would happen to her if anything happened to him? How could he rest knowing that if anything happened to him she'd be left alone, fat and helpless.

"All I want you to do is tell me you'll take care of her. You know she needs somebody. Just promise me you'll always see she's taken care of."

"I will not. Why should I be taking care of your sister. She doesn't even like me and I've already got you to take care of."

"So I suck hind tit, don't I? Not your goddamn family, just George and his sister."

"You aren't your sister."

"Every goddamn week you're sneaking back for your stuck-up bitch mother to hold your goddamn hand and tell you it's all right, you can always come home when you need to. She says that, doesn't she. 'Oh, Marian, you can always come home.' God damn."

"And so what? What's it to you, anyway? At least I've got a real home there."

"You've got your own goddamn house here. You've got a family to take care of here. Why the hell don't you just do it."

"I've got a house here. Well, that's right. That's what I've got, it's a house."

"All I asked you for was a little goddamn feeling for my sister. Well, the hell with you and your mother. You'll goddamn promise me now, and I mean it. Now you goddamn promise me you'll look out for her."

"Not me. Not that great fat thing. Hell no, I won't."

The terrible thing about hearing the voices again is hearing my father's deeply crazed fear of his sister. His fear *for* his sister, really—and for himself. It's like she was a part of him he couldn't bear to look at. He seemed to sense that she was an image of how he'd be, and how he'd finally die.

It's something like self-knowledge, and it goes snaking through everything about him I remember. It's like he had his days carefully filled with alcohol and music and all the time, under it all, the only thing really in motion was the floor, creaking and grinding in one direction.

Almost before my own floor had started to move, he was passing me by like some motorized national monument. I never really knew his pain. He carried his fat, helpless sister in his head like she, and he, were dead and still and alone.

None of it is simple. Nothing about a family is simple except the one, pointed reality that, somewhere along the line, someone has to say, "No more!" and climb out of the machinery.

The Only Thing You Can Do. When you reach that point, there's grace there, though it's hard to see in the clutter. And this is the heart of my clutter, a slight and wavery light at the dead center of the sad and ridiculous tinker toy that I tried to pretend was my personality.

There's a light like the surface of a flaw in a mirror and in it my father is singing to me on a late Saturday morning. I'm lying next to him on the bed in the middle downstairs bedroom where the light is soft because it comes all the way from the front of the house.

I'm rolling toward him, because of his weight, and he's patiently teaching me a song, line by line. Every once in a while he'll call me in and I'll lie down next to his huge, violent presence so it can sing to me, and teach.

Let me get this straight. I'm lying there and his voice is letting me know I'm his son, a little boy who loves *My Wild Irish Rose,* and wants to know the words.

People are complicated, and so are stories. Lie about your feelings in a story and it'll twist under you, like you've stepped on a snake.

THREE

Dead eyes in a moving face are terrible. My father's eyes were starting to die. He always said we lived in the shadow of the asylum. Now the shadow was becoming real. I could see it, and it came from the shadows of real things. Our windows at night threw long, black lines down our lawn, and just past the street lamp they drained off like streams into the real blackness.

Dad's life in music was more or less over. Arthur, his father, owned the beer-hall and Arcade by now, and that's where Dad was working. The end of his life as a professional musician sank him a little deeper into his rage. The alcohol was sinking him anyway. Just a little deeper than the rage was the fear, but we didn't know that until later.

In memory, it seems to me that my father's long coming apart began in earnest just about the time I started school. School had its own shadows, but I much preferred the shadows of the church to my father's.

Saint Mary Magdalen's was on Kingshighway, an open, broad street the trolleys rolled down. Across from it, across from our school, was a marvelous tract of swamp. The school was old, red brick with high, small-paneled windows. It stood by itself on an undersized plot of poorly tended shrubbery.

I started kindergarten in 1937 when I was five. Kindergarten was all right, and I had a good time. Being out of the house was a pleasure. St. Louis was a factional town, and our neighborhood was Catholic. All the kids on my block went to St. Mary Magdalen's. Eugene went, and Jimmy—Joe, Bob Mueller and Harry Book. And JoAnn with her thick black hair.

We all wore the knickers I hated. They made a lousy sound when you walked, the heavy corduroy rubbing and whipping between your thighs. They weren't manly. Neither were raincoats.

We had clubs, secret societies and secret places. Most of all we had secret places. One was a five-foot deep hole we dug down by the brickworks. Another was the treehouse in Jackie and Monte's backyard.

Our clubs were rigidly organized. At the treehouse I was at the bottom of both the pecking order and the tree. I was a sentry. Jackie and Monte had the best guns so they were in charge. They had fake, pearl-handled guns in real leather holsters. Their father was the richest man in the neighborhood. He had racehorses. It was generally true that we didn't know much about each other's parents. That was fine with me.

There were several girls around, but we didn't pay them much attention. Except for Caroline. Caroline had very direct, slate-blue eyes and long, soft hair. She ran our infirmary.

If you got shot you'd fall in slow motion, turning with your ankles crossed and your hands clutched to your chest. Caroline would run to your side and hustle you up to the treehouse, to the hospital. The treatment was always the same. She'd lie you on the floor on your back and straddle you with her head bent and hair falling down. She'd unbutton the fly on your knickers and put her hand in, fumbling around for the bullet. Her hands were always cool.

"Where is it it's deep probably wait a minute I'll just get it don't move I've got it."

I embarrass easily and I always hope that someday she'll find the bullet somewhere else. She never does.

I'm an innocent kid, and pretty gentle. The random images of cruelty are all around, and they clog my head and make me feel trapped. Jackie and Monte like to put bread crumbs on a mouse trap and leave it out for the birds. When the trap closes on a pigeon's neck the neck makes a sound like a snapping twig. If it doesn't die they take it from the trap and tie a two-inch firecracker to its leg.

I remember once they struggled for the pigeon. They'd already lit the firecracker. They threw it just in time, together, with an awkward swoop of tangled arms. The bird was falling while trying to fly, and the firecracker went off just before it hit the ground. I don't think they were particularly vicious kids. It's just how things were. I didn't care much for how things were.

I liked the Roxie a lot. The Roxie was our movie-house. I liked the Arcade at the park too. The first time I went there, Dad took me. It was the Sunday after the frying pan Saturday. It was heaven. He walked me across the airy greenness of the beer garden and into the Arcade, and with my first breath of the old wood I forgave him everything. Maybe he bought me off cheap, but kids are condemned to love their parents anyway. I'd grab at unexpected bits of kindness like the birds did at the crumbs.

On that particular Sunday morning, Dad made me very happy. If I'd known then how much time I'd come to spend in the Arcade, I might have felt differently. As it was, the love I seldom got to use just welled out of me. In the back of my head I thought that maybe I could make a world that would be a cross between Forest Park Highlands and the Roxie. I'd just be very careful with it.

Machines ran into the distance in the long, shadowy hall. Games and peepshows, each with its own billboard. Charlie Chaplin, Fatty Arbuckle and Ben Turpin with crazy eyes. The Chinese Dragon Killer had a corner to itself—burnished metal hand grips and a dream of a Chinese dragon in gilded scales and red and green. There was a machine I blew into and it measured my breath power. When I squeezed the one sprung finger on Uncle Sam's painted metal hand, the machine rated my strength.

Rajah sat in a dusty glass case with a crystal ball and moved stiffly, like an old door. He told your fortune. The multiscopes of follies girls were dreams of innocent pornography, feathered and rounded and soft with smiles.

Next door was the band room, and just outside its long windows that had once fronted the elegant porch of a mansion, the wonderful beer garden. The waiters had moustaches, striped shirts and bright white aprons. Sometimes they sang. The sun came in through the long windows and green trellises. Inside it picked up the machines' brass scrollwork and faded into the corners in a soft, blue-gold powder. The twelve-foot-high and brightly painted clown at the entrance had a big, toothy smile and the word PLAYLAND running from his long, flat shoes to his ruffled collar.

The Roxie, the Arcade and sunlit music in a beer garden. Three ideals.

'38 brings the first grade. School begins in autumn, when the days are getting shorter. I don't like the early dark at all. Every extra minute spent in the living room involves an extra tension. Now I have to come in earlier.

First grade isn't at all like kindergarten. It's overpowering.

Religious instruction begins in the first grade. Events echo in new ways and a threat of corruption is hanging in the air. The nuns are quiet in the halls except for their hard shoes on the marble. They move smoothly with their power in front of them, pale hands folded on their bellies.

Sin and corruption weigh a lot, and I begin to pray furiously. I move into the world of the church with all the timid intensity of a six-year-old emotional exile. School is a world, the outside is a world, and home is a world. When I start to pray it's either at school or in the impossible dark before sleep.

Dad isn't working nights anymore but he's out all night anyway. He usually comes home drunk. He always comes home angry. Mom is drawing power to herself, and the fights are getting one-sided. One-sided or not, they still tear me up. Sometimes in the morning I look hopefully around my classroom for a sign, in someone else's face, of how I feel. I pray that Dad will die, then back off, terrified and sure I've damned myself.

The outside world, outside school and home, has a lot going for it. There are any number of things to do. Bob Mueller and I derail a Kingshighway trolley with blasting caps. When its front wheels hit the caps they blow off their tracks and bounce a little. We're crouched in the weeds by the swamp.

The swamp is a great place. So is the brick factory with its red-domed kilns. All the backyards and alleys have secret places.

Dead things fascinate me.

I'm walking on the tracks of the little railroad and I come upon a dead cat, still between the ties. It's pretty much decomposed but the hard, holdable shapes of the head and teeth keep me in front of it. I gather it up in a box, maggots and all, and take it home to mother.

There's a dead rabbit, too.

I bring it home and match it with another found treasure, a hot water spigot, porcelain and marked with a black "H." I bury the rabbit neatly and set up the spigot crucifix and a cardboard tombstone. "Here Lies Harry," it says.

Caroline had rabbits to bury, but Caroline was an artist. Her Easter rabbit was pregnant when she got her, but all nine babies died the first week. Her mother told her to bury them in the backyard. When she finished she came to get me. Her mother wasn't home and she wanted someone to see them.

In her backyard, right next to the vegetable garden and just above the ground, are nine baby rabbit heads fluffed in a row. "They were so pretty," she said, "I left their heads up." I'm completely filled with admiration.

I get to bury some robins next to my rabbit. I killed them though, and that's different. I didn't want to and the terrible thing was, I couldn't change them being dead.

I was practicing with my BB gun. I was working on a snap-from-the-hip-shot. I aimed at a robin in a nest about three backyards away. I knew I'd never hit it. I did, though, and when I climbed up the tree the robin was dead and there were three babies in the nest. I put them in my shirt and took them home. Two died right away but the third made it.

He never finds out he can fly. He follows me around the ground, very funny-looking and very determined. A workman crosses behind me one morning, on the new back porch they're building, and steps on him. I take him out back and bury him with the others. Burying something you kill is different from burying something you find.

When Harry Book and I become altar boys we get to serve Requiem Masses. It's great. We get to go to the cemetery in a limousine and afterwards, always, we get folding money pressed in our hands by the mortician.

Being an altar boy is one of the ways to slip the nuns. We

serve every Sunday and all through Lent. We're familiars of awful mysteries. We have prestige. The habit of a nun is an untouchable barrier, but the cassock of a priest is mystery itself. We have access to the Sacristy and we're skilled ringers of the bells.

Harry isn't a lively kid. He's stocky, blond and serious. We get along fine. Sometimes he takes me out to his father's garage where the beautiful 1927 Chrysler with the wooden spokes is resting between its rare outings. Harry loves the car and the way it smells in the dark. We all love it.

The first year as altar boys is bright. The school is mostly downhill from Winona, and in the winter we can sled almost all the way. We get up good speed. Cars are high enough to sled under. Harry doesn't show much emotion, but after a good sled run he gets a strange, flowery expression on his face. His eyes are unusually bright through his glasses and his cheeks are windblown red. I really like Harry.

It's Harry who first thinks of drinking the communion wine. We're in the sacristy before mass, pouring the wine in the cruet. He stops with the bottle in the air.

"Hey, Jack, we could drink this if we wanted."

"Yeah?"

"No one'll know."

"Did you ever drink wine?"

"Sure, lots of times."

"You go first."

Harry almost giggles. This is a different Harry. He takes the cruet in both hands, carefully, and drinks with little sips. He can't spill any, not on his chest.

"Is it good?"

"Sure it's good."

He gives me the cruet and I drink.

He finishes what's left and we somberly refill it. The wine was sweet and heady.

It's wonderful.

Father Malachi is dark and quiet, with a vicious temper. He always wants the cruet filled to the top. In the mornings, he shakes.

In my class I drift like a mist in my chair. We served the mass through the haze of the wine. The red of the wine that's the blood, and the raised arms, and the bell. I was a secret. I was a secret watcher. I wasn't Jack Erdmann, I was a secret watcher with a warm belly. Jack's miracle. The unromantic reality is that all through Lent at St. Mary Magdalen's school in 1939, mass was celebrated daily by a hungover priest and two drunk eight-year-olds.

My mother had no idea. She was purely thrilled to see me at the altar. My mother's mother saw it as a sign that even George Erdmann's unregenerate genes were no match for the Holy Ghost. My first experience with the spiritual. Misery spreads away from that chapel like real blood. The spirit is tinged with the blankness of nuns, the rawness of Dad's hands and my own drunkenness.

It's a shame. Children are naturally reverent. They feel awe. My world was a blur of mystery and reverence, and from Caroline's tender rabbit-heads to the solemn presence of Harry's father's Chrysler, my emotions went out perfectly, like real prayer.

Sitting in chapel at St. Mary Magdalen's, it was like the light was coming from so far away that when it finally reached me there was just enough left to make a lonely kid wonder whether or not he'd really seen the Virgin move her eyes. It was too bad. Because I had serious things to think about, and serious gaps in my head.

My greatest awe was of my father, but I also wanted him dead. I didn't think I could bring that to church.

The things I heard weren't always useful. "God helps those

who help themselves." I heard that a lot. The kid who acts on it is in for some serious trouble.

Mrs. Connolly is a widow and has a garage she never uses. It's full of displaced things, so many stored and forgotten things that the space inside it rises like a teepee. On the days when there aren't any kids around and there isn't anything I'm expected to do, I go to Mrs. Connolly's garage, climb in through a window, and play that it *is* a teepee.

I like to light fires too. I love it when they let me light the fire in the backyard's square, concrete-lined ash-pit.

So I light a fire in Mrs. Connolly's garage. It's a small fire, just right for a wigwam, but it makes enough smoke to bring the fire engines and my mother. Dad isn't home so I'm sent to my room. Downstairs I can hear the clicking drawl of the telephone. Dad uses his hands when he's angry, but when the punishment is considerable, he uses his right slipper on my bare ass.

Now all I can do is wait. I watch the light fade on the other side of my window.

"God helps those who help themselves."

I go quietly to Dad's room and steal his right slipper. Mom is in the living room now, and the radio is on. I tiptoe down the stairs and out the back screen door. There's a shovel on the ground near the ash-pit, and I dig a little hole for the slipper. Around the ash-pit, rats have made tunnels to get to the garbage. Maybe they'll eat it. Even if they don't, he'll never find it. When I finish I feel like I've been holding my breath for days. I go back in quietly, and up the stairs.

Dad comes home. The first thing he says is, "Where is the little son-of-a-bitch?"

I hear him on the stairs.

"Where's my goddamn slipper?"

He breaks through my door and hits me once on the side

of my head. He drags me out and down the stairs in a whirl-wind of hands.

"Now, you rotten little son-of-a-bitch, now you'll tell me where that slipper is."

He hits me with his half-closed fist and I fall backwards over the footstool.

I guess I'm crying. All I know is how his hands come out of the air. He's in between me and the floor lamp and the light is broken and confused. I take him to the slipper and he digs it up. It's packed with damp earth. I'm standing behind him in the almost-dark with my arms folded and shaking on my chest.

"God damn," he says, "god damn."

Back in the house he beats me with his belt. After that it's always the belt. He always comes home so angry. I know he's working at the Arcade and I don't understand why he's so angry. I know the Arcade doesn't seem the same anymore.

Mom knows I have to be punished. She hates it, but she knows it has to be done. When the beatings are for no reason, she leaves the room. She can't stand to see it.

She only joined in once.

That was one of my few bits of predictability, that Mom wouldn't join in. But this time it's almost Christmas and sometimes they ask me what I want. I really don't know. I don't know why I don't know, I just don't. Probably I think there's a right and a wrong answer. Christmas Eve we're in the living room. Pat's doing the dishes and I'm on the floor with a book. I look up, and out of nowhere I say, "I could use some more track for my train."

There's a live, edgy silence and then, behind me, my mother says, "*Damn* you."

The beating comes mostly from Dad, but Mom helps a little. He uses a rolled-up St. Louis telephone book.

I've already done a lot of praying, but now I start with a

vengeance. I'm going to take the wine-warm Sunday mornings and the blueness and fleshy gentleness of the Virgin and
make them the stuff of my life. I'm not a worldly kid.

I do have fun in the streets and God knows I did get to
blow a trolley off its tracks, but in the part of me I think of
as the real me, my interests are purely spiritual.

Not spiritual, really, but magical. I'm not being spiritual,
I'm trying to make magic. I just don't know the difference.

FOUR

"Harry? Hey, if we're drinking this wine it's a mortal sin and makes it so we have to go to hell."

"Yeah but the wine didn't get consecrated yet. If it was consecrated and we took it we'd have to go to hell."

"But it's Father Malachi's wine we're stealing."

"It isn't either his. It's the church's."

"Stealing is a mortal sin."

"Stealing is when you take something and keep it for money or something."

"Well, we're taking it and we're not giving it back."

"Well, we're not keeping it."

"But we're not giving it back."

"Okay then, then you don't get any."

"Well this is the last time."

"How come you don't confess if you're so scared."

"Father Malachi hears my confession."

"So? He hears mine too."

"Yeah, I know. He'd kill us."

"It doesn't matter when you confess as long as you do it sometime."

"We could wait 'til we're out of St. Mary Magdalen's. We could wait 'til we get a different priest."

"It's really a long time to confess about."

"You have to say how many times."

"Three years. Damn."

"Three years isn't even how many times. Three years is how long. It's four times a month. Whatever four times a month for three years is."

"Twelve months makes it 48 times a year."

"That's too many."

"There's no such thing as too many when you confess."

"Forty-eight times a year is like you're not sorry."

"When you confess it makes you sorry. Even murder. Like a long time ago. You can confess anything."

"Yeah."

"So it's okay."

"I just figure maybe since it's church stuff we stole we'll still go to hell."

"Sister Mary Barbara says there's only the one sin against the Holy Ghost that confession isn't any good for you and you don't even know what it is."

"So. So you don't know either."

"I think they tell us when we graduate but we have to promise not to tell."

"Maybe it's drinking the wine."

"It couldn't be 'cause it's got to be worse than murder."

"Yeah."

"Anyway, it's getting late. I'll pour, you get the cruet."

"Okay. You know we better not die before we get to High School."

"Even if you do you have to make sure you have a priest there."

"Yeah."

With the wine comes a certain lightness, and now I'm lost in the magic, an elegant mix of lightness and physical centering. It moved my center out of my head and into my belly. It felt better there.

I pray strenuously to my foot-high, ghostly-plaster crucifix. I won it for selling Maryknoll stamps. It has a lovely white glow to it, next to my bed. I'm meticulous, and if I get even one word of a prayer wrong, I start again from the beginning.

Most of all I'm alone in the dark. The dark behind the pale white cross and Jesus is hell. I know a lot about hell. I hear about it all the time. In hell the time moves very slowly. Eternity means nothing to me, but time moving slowly does. Eternity is just a flat wall my thinking won't go past. The way they tell it is with all the grains of sand on the beach. If every grain of sand on the beach is equal to a thousand years you can go through every one of them and when you're finished your stay in hell will have just begun.

And the fire burns just like a fire here. But you can't get away from it, ever.

The good thing is the Virgin doesn't seem to have much to do with hell. Neither does Jesus, and I pray they'll get between God and me.

On top of everything else, I've begun to fall in love.

The first time it's Maggie, a public school girl. I meet her at the Arcade on a weekend, and right away we get along without being embarrassed. She has a soft, round face and olive skin. Her hair is very black. She has a plain gold bracelet on her left wrist. She turns it a lot with her other hand.

Sometimes I meet her coming home from school and we walk together. We don't have much to say. At school they say the public school kids are going to hell. I never mention that.

On a Fall afternoon that's a little misty we walk home holding hands. I'm choking with excitement and every once in a while I slip the bracelet up her wrist with my other hand 'til it binds softly.

I know absolutely nothing about sex.

My father never tells me anything and my mother seems like she doesn't know anything. Bob Mueller tries to explain it to me on an afternoon in the swamp. I don't get it. My penis is what I piss with. Going home from the swamp in the twilight I feel angry and resentful. He's given me a dark, unpleasant image. As I understand it, sex involves mutual, internal urination. I wouldn't do that to Maggie. My father would probably do something like that. I don't want to think about it. Down by the brickworks, the guys sing dirty songs. I sing along but they all know I'm faking it.

I'm a very scrawny kid. Scrawny and innocent. But I don't get picked on. I seem to be able to back people off with my eyes. I don't see Dad much. He's out and drunk most every night.

This is when I dream I'm having a nightmare. I wake up in the dream. Mom and Dad are standing by my bed and Mom says, "You had a bad dream." They take me downstairs with my pillow and blanket. Dad keeps his hand on my shoulder all the way down. It's very real.

We go to the small bedroom, the one Dad lay in when he sang to me, and they put me to bed. I push myself in under the covers and settle into an easy curve. I start to fade out but something isn't right. My eyes open up and, as if they were ears, I can suddenly hear the laughing. In the dark at the foot of the bed Mom and Dad are laughing at me. The only light in the room is on their faces, and their faces aren't quite right. They're the same, but changed. There's a little gap before I understand. Then the pain hits like something inside me is being forced open.

When I wake up, in my own bed, I wake up in a rage. I think it really happened and I stomp down the stairs, still a little asleep, and demand to know why they laughed at me. Mom's at the sink and looks at me strangely.

"You just had a dream, Jack. That's all. Nobody laughed at you. Whyever would I laugh at you?"

I stand there and finally say, "Oh."

On a Saturday morning he's badly hungover and the left corner of his lower lip is drooping like it always does when he's real sick. I haven't mentioned his lower lip. It lets me know how dangerous he is at any time. When it droops like this he'll only get violent if I actually do something. When it's pushed all the way out it's dangerous just to be near him.

We're at the Arcade and I forget to wind a row of machines at the far end of the hall. The heavy iron crank we wind them with is black and handle-bent like a car crank. It weighs three or four pounds and now, as he yells, "You little son-of-a-bitch," I look up and see it cutting through the air in odd loops. It rings when it hits a machine and thunks when it lands. This is something new, and the fear gets inside to hook up with something bigger.

"Hey, Mom?"

"Yes."

"I wanted to ask you something about Dad."

"Why don't you ask him? Whatever it is I'm sure he knows much better."

"I can't."

"Well? What is it?"

"It's when I was at the Arcade something happened."

"Okay, Jack."

"What happened was he threw the big wind-up crank and almost hit me."

"Oh Jack, he probably didn't see you. He probably wanted it out of his way and he didn't see where you were."

"No, he yelled 'You little son-of-a-bitch' and threw it at me and it hit one of the machines."

"The crank you mean. That goes in the side and you wind with?"

"Yeah."

"Well I'll have to ask him about it. That's awfully heavy, isn't it?"

"Yeah. But that's not what I wanted to ask you. I mean I don't want you to say anything to Dad about it."

"Yes?"

"I wanted to ask you if you think Dad might ever want to kill me."

"Oh, Jack, no. How can you say that? He'd never want that, that's the last thing he'd want."

"He gets that way and I feel like he might kill me."

"No, Jack. That's so silly I can't tell you."

"He doesn't do things to Pat."

"Well, Pat is a girl and she's quieter. She doesn't get into as much mischief."

"He doesn't want to kill me for doing something."

"Now stop it, Jack. Nobody's going to kill you and that's the end of it."

"Dad hits me harder than the nuns and they use rulers and stuff."

"I don't want to hear any more. George has his weaknesses like all of us but I think if we just try to understand him things will be a lot better for everyone. You know if his father had been more like a real father then maybe George wouldn't have been such a Mama's boy. It's a terrible thing and I'm sure he doesn't want it to happen to you so sometimes he's a little bit hard on you. There are a lot of things you don't understand and I think if you pray for all of us, and your father especially, I'm sure that would help."

"I do pray for him."

(God knows I do.)

"That's wonderful, Jack, and I'm very proud of you."

"He loves Pat."

"He loves all of us."

Whatever she says to me now, it finally becomes clear that she heard what I was saying. This is late in 1941. By March of '42, Mom had Dad sober. It took a lot. It took another downtown girlfriend, and nights of shrieking and screaming, but when she finally got us all packed and the luggage was waiting on the steps for the taxi that would take us to her mother's, George went sullenly to his doctor, came home, and gave up drinking. Safe at last in the hands of the professionals.

Things change. My physical fear of him still rustles around in my chest, but the fact is he isn't nearly as likely to swing at me. I even work with him at the Arcade on a regular basis. Maggie and her family have moved to Kansas City and I miss her a lot, especially at the Arcade. But not having to feel like he wants to kill me does a lot for my mood.

I work at the Arcade a lot more. There are guys all over Forest Park Highlands the public rarely gets to see. They're seedy and inbred. They work behind the scenes, and they're pure Carny cynics. The Carny men are students of human vanity, and their coldness is perfect. The only kindness they show is, if they like you, they'll teach you some things. When they do it's like being invited into a bad-smelling clubhouse. My innocence tickles them.

In order to get from the Arcade to the bathroom, I have to pass through the bandroom. The bandroom is where they hang out to drink and play cards. I don't like going through it while they're there. Shy doesn't cover how they make me feel. When I do go through I'm consciously stiff. Some days I hold off going to the bathroom 'til I can't stand it, and race through.

There's one afternoon when I open up the bandroom door

and it's dark inside, with crackly light. There are only two windows and they've been covered over with army blankets. When I get inside the projector is whirring right next to me.

They're watching a movie. I close the door quietly. The movie is all brown and yellowish-white, and until I get balanced the shapes are confused. When I sort them out they're two bellies and the tops of four legs. The scene opens up and I can see it's a man and a woman, both naked. Mortal sin hits me in the throat.

The woman is bent back on a messed-up bed with her feet still touching the floor. The man is leaning over her, holding himself off the bed with straight arms. He has socks on. Their bodies are real close below their bellies and they're pumping up and down and back and forth right at that spot, below their bellies. Sometimes the woman's legs jump out wider, then come back in. Her head is going back and forth and her hands go up and down in time. The only sound is crackling. Johnny's in the back and when he sees me he laughs.

"Hey Jackie, how *about* that? Gonna be like your old man, huh? Get you some of your old man's pussy, huh?"

I put my hands in my pockets and walk down the side wall to the bathroom. They're all laughing now.

"Hey Jackie, what ya' got in ya' pocket, kid?"

I stay in the bathroom for a long time. Walking back isn't so bad because in the glare from the projector I can't see. It makes me feel like they can't see me. I turn at the door again and the woman is face down with the man on his knees and holding her around the waist.

"How about it, Jackie? You like it that way?"

I go back into the light of the Arcade with my legs rigid and shaky. I leave the Arcade at twilight.

Virginia Ascher, Mom's old dancing partner, comes over for dinner. Dad sits sober at the table. He looks like he's counting his chews. Mom and Virginia chatter about the old days. After dinner they turn on the radio and try out some old steps.

They could ask Dad to play for them, but that's risky. They stand turned sideways with left arms out, then count and catch the beat for an awkward start. They have a little, almost soft-shoe interlude that they almost remember. They hitch their skirts and drift a bit in a circle, lightly. Sometimes they look at their feet.

Dad says and does nothing.

Mom always pulls up her skirt too high. Virginia's is up to mid-thigh but Mom's is higher, barely below her underwear. It makes me crazy when she does that. She shouldn't, especially not tonight. I want to run away and hide. I want to not have to look at her thighs and bright smile.

Dad gets up from his chair with his paper and goes to his room. I go back to the dining room table and make wet circles on the polish with the bottom of a water glass. Pat comes home from her girlfriend's house. She spends a lot of time at her friends' houses. She throws her books on the table and slips right in with the women.

"What the hell," I consciously think.

1942.

I follow the war as if it were a serial. Three doors down is an older couple with three blue stars on the glass of their parlor window. The curtain is always drawn behind them. A blue star means a son in the war. One day one of the stars is gold. Two weeks later and they're all gold. A gold star means a dead son. The curtain always stays closed. I wonder how they must feel. They must have changed the stars at night, when no one could see. It makes me feel sad.

Dad is getting heavier, seriously heavy. His lower lip doesn't stick out any more, it just droops. He seems to be moving more slowly, and taking smaller steps.

The whole year is full of deep images. When I see Dad without his clothes on all the definition has gone from his body, he's shapeless fat. Somehow the father who terrorized me has gone to sleep in this huge, fleshy pod. His flesh swells around his dead eyes.

I don't know where he's gone. I wanted to be proud of him, and I wanted him to love me, and I wanted him dead. But all he did was go away. He just isn't there. He takes the pills the doctor gave him. He takes a lot of them. I know because he sends me to the drug store to get him more. None of us know what's happening.

I get back from school one day and he's sitting in his living room chair. He's leaning forward with his arms dangling down between his legs and touching the floor.

He's sobbing big, wet, broken sobs.

I go over and stand in front of him with my books under my arm. His head is lower than the piano keyboard. He tips it back on his neck and looks at me.

"I can't stand it, Jack. I'm so goddamn miserable I just can't stand it."

He's never talked to me this way before. I put my books on the floor and crouch in front of him.

"I'd rather be dead. I'm lower than whale shit, Jack."

It's not even like he's talking to me. It doesn't even matter. My father's in there somewhere and he's trying to reach me. I hear myself say, with a different voice, "I love you dad. Everything'll be all right." He doesn't hear me.

"I'm scared, Jack. I think all the time I want to be dead but I'm scared."

He's looking straight at me and his eyes look sore.

"Thank God you're here. You understand me, don't you, Jack?"

"Sure."

He puts out his left hand, without straightening up, and I take it.

"I'm just so goddamn miserable."

Two days later his mother dies.

She isn't supposed to die. She's the cotter pin that holds George's mind together—her now-and-forever ampleness. She goes so deep in him that he's never bothered to hide the attachment. Another man might have been a little embarrassed at having to live so close to his mother, but not Dad. To Dad it was just a fact and he didn't give a damn who knew it. He was a little prince, and anything that might have struck an outsider as unusual was, in George's mind, a perfectly ordinary bit of Royal Family Reality.

The asylum we lived in the shadow of was on Arsenal. It was run by the state. You could tell what it was from two blocks away. It rose up out of its lot like a brick head with windows for eyes. To me and the other kids it was a fortress. It might as well have had metal bands cinching it in. Craziness was dark and metallic.

The day after Martha's funeral we went to the asylum for the first time. It was a Wednesday and a heavy, old, dull grey from the moment I woke up. Downstairs I could hear Mom. She was saying the Hail Mary over and over again. Behind her voice I could hear Dad crying.

Downstairs I stand in the arched entrance to the living room. Dad's in his chair and crying from way down. Mom's sitting on a footstool next to him and holding his hand. She's still saying the Hail Mary. When she stops Dad grabs her hand tighter and she starts again. Mom looks up and says, "The doctor's on his way, Jack. You better get dressed."

Dad's car is a black, ugly, '39 Chevy. We drive him to the asylum but we don't get to go in, not today. The four corner towers of the asylum are the four points of a square crown on a square, brick head.

When we get home Pat's on the telephone with Mom's mother. Mom takes over and Pat and I sit down at the kitchen table and eat cookies in a thick silence.

Dad's in for two weeks and six shock treatments. We get to visit three days before they're going to let him out.

Our house has been full of relatives. My mother's mother is there all the time. She's very dignified. Much too dignified for "I told you so." Father Mullally comes by from the parish. He tells us that before the first shock treatment Dad had asked to be baptized. He was sure he was going to die. The priest asked him if he'd continue in the church when he got out and Dad said no. He just didn't want to go to hell. The priest refused him.

On a Tuesday we all get back in the Chevy and head out for our visit.

Dad's on the second floor. There are inmates drifting in the cream and dark-wood hallway. They pay us no mind. It's another grey day and Dad looks drained and mountainous in the flat light. He doesn't really recognize us. His last treatment was yesterday. Grandmother stays by the door in her fox stole with the little heads. We stay for an hour or so. Mom holds his hand and talks about nothing. He moves his eyes without turning his head, and sometimes she dabs at his mouth with her handkerchief.

On the way home no one says anything. As we get out of the car Mom takes my arm and says, "You're praying, Jack, aren't you?"

We pick him up Thursday. He's a lot livelier. He's still not quite there, but he is animated. As a matter of fact he makes loud sexual advances to Mom in the back seat. I surprise myself when I laugh. I can't help it. I'm choking trying to keep it down. I'm eleven years old and I've started to see things from the outside.

Jack, I think, was a pretty nice kid.

FIVE

I figure it's about time I had some fun. In 1946 I'm a certified teenager. I'll be one for a very long time. I live in a swirl of blunders, good intentions and fleshy dreams. I could use some real fun. I'm going to be a student for the next eight years. There's never been any doubt about college. I'm going to college. I'm not worried about it. I'll be out of the house more than I've ever been before. I like that. The house is a wound that doesn't heal.

Fun isn't exactly the word for what I have in mind. Football stardom, literary distinction, personal sanctity and the slow moves of a full-bodied woman getting out of silk. I'm a romantic and I have all of the weaknesses and most of the strengths of the romantic teenager. The strengths aren't trivial. We see a lot, we have a lot of endurance, and our emotions are at least jumbled around real mysteries—old, bloody and deep.

My goal, as always, is to make it to the other side where things are different. So I go to the places where we think the secrets are kept. The pool room is down on Grand and Alberta. It's filled to the windows with fine, green, powdery light that seems to me to open onto a wild-side paradise. It's an opening, and openings are a lot on my mind.

The six old, green tables are bright rectangular clearings in the haze, and the small bar in the front has a flawed mirror and a bank of almost-working neon signs. Sometimes half a sign will buzz and flash on.

S ag eer, Gr ese ck, dweiser

Before we found the pool hall we'd cut school to fish at the lake. I'm reading *Huckleberry Finn* and trying on the part. That's the sort of thing I do. At night I writhe and try to talk to God, and in the morning I pick out an attitude, try it on, and see what the traffic will bear.

The pool hall is better than fishing. It's a wonderland of possibility. With a cue in your hand you can really strike some poses. You can practice, and we practice everything. We try out masculine stances. We pretend to unflappability. We start to get the rhythms of our obscenities down. If you don't have the rhythm, you might as well forget it.

"Goddamn shit," we say, "son-of-a-bitch five *move* it, *damn,* get legs."

Clank and thunk.

Chauncey is a cripple who hangs around the tables. He's slightly retarded but shoots good pool. We're not good enough to be hustleable, but Chauncey could do it if we were. We wouldn't feel good about being hustled by a retarded cripple. We have a lot of work to do. Our whole world exists in that heightened atmosphere where everything seems important, and everything has a point.

Twilight isn't my best time of day. I'm walking home from the pool hall. I think I'll stay in my room tonight. I'll listen to the radio. *Inner Sanctum* is on. St. Mary Magdalen's goes by in the weak light. It's a dark, heavy building but it looks like a toy. It's like a toy building next to my electric train track. Sometimes things look funny at twilight. Walking home is plain sad.

I'm angry at the way I am. Jesus, there's something wrong with me. Other kids don't do this. I know they don't. I cross the street. I'd like it if all the houses were lit up already. I know I'm not afraid, it's just that I feel everything in this light is changed for the worse. It's my fault. It's the way I am.

The light is just nowhere. It doesn't make anything bright and the shadows aren't real dark yet. It feels better when all the house-lights are on. Caroline moved and her house is still dark. I wish I had some idea how the other kids feel. I wish I could find out. This is stuff we never talk about.

Mom and Pat are in the kitchen and Dad is downstairs. The live music is over but he still has his records. *Davenport Blues* comes up the stairs. It's Bix's solo, very shiny and sad.

I go to my room and turn on the radio. It seems like a real teenager's room. What I think my room should look like. In the back of my closet is an old *Esquire* with a great Vargas girl in it. She's barely into one of those filmy black things, and she's looking at me over her shoulder. Franklin Roosevelt is over my desk. Half a B-17 model is tilted in its parts box.

I'm going to South Side High. Mom didn't want me to, but I did anyway. Bob Mudd is my hero and he's captain of the South Side football team. I'm sure I'm going to be a football star. Size has nothing to do with it. It's a matter of being born special. With Bob Mudd there I can't miss.

It turns out, of course, that I'm not a football star. South Side is a disaster. It's tough and low-class and all I can do is try to let it pass me by. It pretty much does. The thing I'll remember most about South Side is sitting next to Jerry Brangan. He's fresh out of reform school. The word is that he was in for having sex with his sister. The word also is that he's still having sex with his sister.

This is mortal sin with a vengeance. I watch him like a hawk for some telltale sign of damnation. One morning he's slowly dragging one of his big thumbs up and down the erection that bulges on his inner thigh. What'll he do if he has to stand up? Doesn't he care?

"You fuckin' got something to look at?"

"Me? No, nothing, no."

At the end of the year I move on. St. Louis University High School isn't hugely expensive but it's the only available private school for the sons of the Catholic rich. At South Side I was able to skate but it won't be like that anymore. At South Side I had a 98 average and the Jesuits are very happy to pick me up as a transfer. I'm probably a genius.

It's autumn and autumn is powerful. The physical sadness of it, and the way its colors seep and leak. This particular autumn is all promises. Everything folds and slides and smudges-in around the soft body, in soft clothes, of a girl I haven't met yet.

They pass me on the street and their skirts are swinging on their hips like bells. They have bendable waists and their legs are firm and soft at the same time. Under their skirts the legs widen steadily into the thighs I never get to see. I can feel the muscles of my own though, and I know they can feel theirs, the widest parts of them rubbing as they walk. Everything is erotic. There's a distant, misted tension between their mouths and their bellies—something receding, and powerful.

At home I have a perfect sister, a mother who's slowly disappearing into the stony mazes of the Church, and a father who tends the Arcade, threatens me, gets fatter and sometimes sobs uncontrollably as I cradle his head in my arms and tell him what he wants to hear about God and the Virgin Mary. I have two lives and they're separating. In the one I want to live, my romanticism is running wild. My groin is stirring like church drapery in a soft, steady breeze.

I need to do something. I need to unlock the world. The night I steal the port I find the key. Dad has a couple of bottles of port on a high shelf in a downstairs closet. He never was much of a wine drinker. They've been there for years. Friday night the house is empty. Mom and Pat are spending the night at her mother's. Dad is in the hospital again.

I go downstairs for the bottles at six. Joe Hagerty is coming by to drink with me. I put both bottles and a couple of water glasses on the little table by the door. He comes in about a quarter after. He's a big, easygoing kid, but tonight he looks shifty. His hands are in his pockets and his shoulders are riding too high.

"You got it?"

"Sure I've got it. I said I would."

I point at the table and Joe picks up a bottle as if he were knowledgeable. It's a great label. It's a man in a dark cape in a wide, drooping black hat. Both his hands are out in front of him offering a bunch of dark grapes.

"I never drank port before."

"You probably never drank anything."

"Yeah, I did, my old man's Rock 'n Rye once."

"You get much?"

"Not really. He watches the bottles. My mother watches the bottles too. Her old man was a drunk."

"Yeah. Well my old man never drinks this stuff. He doesn't even look at it. It looks like it makes a stain."

"Why would I spill it?"

"We just have to be careful."

"Where is everybody?"

"They're at my grandmother's."

"Can I turn on the radio?"

"Sure."

The Shadow is on.

"The weed of crime bears bitter fruit."

Maybe so. The port, though, is sweet. And right after it's sweet there's a beautiful little burning that flattens it out, and cleans your mouth. It's a magic feeling. It's like you're finally putting something *real* in your mouth; something that will do things. Screw the communion wine. When half of it's gone, we're well past the giggling stage.

"This is pretty good stuff, you know."

"If we could get some we could hide it somewhere safe. We could hide it down by the swamp somewhere."

"We could hide it in the Sacristy."

"How'd you know about that?"

"Harry told me."

"Yeah, we could put it in one of those giant bottles in the back." We're getting bored and ridiculous. The thing is now, we need to get out and show the world just what kind of guys we really are.

There's an old canteen in the pantry, the round, flat kind, and I fill it with the rest. I don't spill a drop. Joe has a big inside pocket in his coat. On the edge of danger, we're poised and shrewd. We almost never go to dances. But tonight is different. Tonight we're going to the CYO dance at St. Mary Magdalen.

The light comes out the front doors at St. Mary Magdalen with a kind of glory. Shadows are moving through it and slice bits off like the lights of headlights do on my bedroom ceiling. We flatten on the wall next to the steps and down some more port. We don't check our coats. The girl at the door to the gym doesn't care. She's bored and lonely. We stand in the doorway and blink in the colored light.

On the dance floor our presence is crackling through the crowd. The guys are interested and the girls are murmuring. Heads are turned. Probably half the guys at the dance have liquor stashed somewhere. But this is different. This is flaunting it.

So we're standing there and pretty soon it starts to feel like we should *do* something.

"What the hell do we do now?"

Joe's voice is too loud.

"Do whatever you like."

"Sure, great, why didn't I think of that?"

Everybody knows. There are glances and shudders slipping from one couple to the next. A girl gliding by says, "That's disgusting, how could they come here like that?" I jam my hands in my pockets and lean back on my heels a little. Disgusting is my middle name. Joe's coat slips off his arm and clanks on the wood floor. There's a flurry on the left side of the gym. Father Martin is bearing down on us. It's best to get out.

I give the crowd a benediction with my right hand and we lope down the hall. We were only there for five minutes, only in the doorway. But something happened and I can feel it. It doesn't matter what the dancing girls are saying, the central fact is that they're talking about us. About me. In the turning colored lights women are whispering about me.

I can see the outlines of another world.

My mood has gone tender and delicate. The music is still in my head. I wish I could walk a little better but I know that all I need is practice. This isn't the goddamn communion wine, this is real. We walk slowly and raggedly home. Joe stays for a while. He chews Sen-Sen by the handful. I check his breath before he leaves. It seems fine to me.

I turn on the radio and sit in Dad's chair with my feet up. The rosy, floral print looks good to me. Jo Stafford is singing *I'll Be Seeing You.* "In everything that's bright and gay." Her voice is in that beautiful, middle-reed register. I love music.

St. Louis U High is going to be a bitch. I don't care. It's

like *Gone With The Wind*. I always loved that comfortable "Tomorrow is another day." Right now I'm on top of everything. I'll do whatever I have to do. I'm centered. When I go to bed the sheets are warm and sentimental. I sleep deeply and well, without dreams. In the morning the sun is out and I'm not sick.

That's the greatest thing. I'm not sick.

S I X

There are things to look forward to now. There's a bar on a dead line between home and St. Louis U High. It's called The Savoy. It's on Dago Hill. The cops choose not to notice it. Teenagers drink there. Most of the St. Louis U High student body drinks there. When the beat cop comes in he leaves with a sandwich, a bottle in a brown paper bag and a five dollar bill. They have a garden restaurant, and the bar is old wood. Beers are a dime.

There are booths, but it's mostly the social drinkers who use them. Boring guys who talk about classes. They drink slow, and as far as the guys at the bar are concerned they're middle-aged already. We're different at the bar. At four in the afternoon on a weekday, three or four of us are drinking seriously. We don't spend much time standing. We sit and hunch a little. It takes about three beers for me to start to feel easy. I feel the beginnings of charm after three. All I have to worry about is the present. I'm right here.

This isn't the Jack Erdmann who looks out of his head like a mouse out of a jack 'o lantern. It isn't the other one either, the one the doctor at the asylum described as the only sixty-five-year-old adolescent he'd ever come across. This is the centered Jack Erdmann. I feel it in my gut and my emotions cluster around in a warm, comfortable ball.

My new school persona is complete. I'm the nice guy who tries real hard but can't quite cut it. I'm not really up to the work but my mediocrity is honest and forthright. There's no way to fault me. I'm devout, and I'm trying as hard as I can. The faculty respects me for that.

"Fuck school," I think at the bar.

Not only do I have my act worked out, I have a secret friend to help me bring it off. Alcohol is my friend and in 1948, in St. Louis, I'm able to buy his time, fifteen or not. The bottles are arranged on glass shelves. Right in front of the mirror. The mirror is long and ornate, and set in rosewood. The labels on the bottles have solid designs in luxurious colors. When I look in the mirror behind them I'm seeing myself *now*. At the bar. My glass goes up and down and I can't say I'm worried. My teachers have names like Black Mike Hindelang. Fuck it. I know how to drink. I drink steadily and I don't get out of control. King Harrigan gets out of control and he's sixteen. He doesn't really get out of control when he's conscious. It's just that he passes out every night. He's a diabetic. That must have something to do with it. Vince Frynn gets out of control. He eats chalk and drinks ink. Bill Manetti is out-of-control angry. I can tell. It's not anything he does. I can just feel it. I figure I see a lot. He's really lonely. I'm one of his only friends. I watch him when the guys are talking about going somewhere. He stays on the side because he's sure we won't ask him. He's not popular. But his father is. His father gives parties and lets us drink. Whiskey sours. I don't really care about complicated mixed drinks. I like Manhattans, though. Harrigan drinks boilermakers. Drafts and shots of Kessler's rye. Smmoooth as silk.

The Fathers could probably close The Savoy if they wanted to. The Fathers are Jesuits though, and drinking isn't nearly the threat to the soul that lust is. Lust is an animal. It eats your head. That's how they see it. Lust is on their minds a lot. Drinking is just what men do. Lust is kind of a tame word for what I feel. I study myself in the mirror. I'm not bad looking but I look even younger than I am. I know that. So I'm fifteen. I've been here for three hours and I can still walk and talk all right. Better. I have a quick tongue and I'm a good mimic. I wish I looked older. I wish there were more girls in the Savoy. I wish some girl would come in and ask me to take her home. She'd be wearing a white skirt tight halfway up her hips, and I could slide my hands up under it. I don't care about lust. Lust is something adults have. Mary wears just that kind of white skirt. She has a beautiful body and lots of soft, hanging sweaters. I need another drink. How many guys can drink like I can? Two more will do it. How many guys in here are writing a novel? Things are going to get better by themselves. I don't have to do anything. All I have to do is wait. They'll come to me. She'll let me kiss her breasts and more. It's only five o'clock. I have enough for two more. This time Mel isn't going to hit on me for money. This goes for my last drink.

"No," I say, and toast myself in the mirror.

I've just about learned the first axiom of the alcoholic discipline.

The Pain Can Be Killed.

Its first corollary is waiting in the wings.

Kill The Pain At All Cost.

I'm not doing well, but I am getting by, and getting by is all I'm interested in. I was interested in being an athlete, but clearly I'm not one. If you could get a letter for drinking I'd have it made. They should give letters for drinking. It's at least as difficult, and just as manly, as any sport. Holding your liquor is one of the manly arts and drinking well confers a worldly distance. I'm not an achiever, I'm an aristocrat.

The fact is there's more distinction in holding your liquor well than in getting laid. It's better to handle your liquor and not get laid than it is to get laid and not be able to handle your liquor. Sooner or later we'll all get laid, but a guy who can't drink without making a fool of himself will probably be that way for the rest of his life.

Going to dances is easy now. Things start to happen when I discover that if you're drinking, and apart, girls will find you interesting. All that's required is that you be there, hold your liquor, and look deep. Mary comes to me.

She's going with Ed Kreisler, a big guy, a junior, and a football star. But when I'm standing by myself near the refreshment table, she brushes up against me. I hold my breath.

"*You* look sad. Do I know you?"

"I doubt it. I see you a lot though."

The bourbon talks easily.

"*I* see *you*. You're by yourself a lot."

"When I feel like it."

"Are you with somebody now?"

"No. Some of the guys."

"Always the other guys, huh?"

"I like the music. I didn't come to dance."

"Are you a musician?"

"A little."

"I love music."

"You love Kenton?"

"Sure."

"He'll be at Forest Park Highlands next week."

"Are you asking me?"

"Sure."

"What night?"

"Friday."

Ed is looming through the crowd.

"I'd like that."

She puts her hand on my arm.

"You know you're cute, don't you?"

Jesus.

I don't. But I'll fake it.

So next Friday night, Mary of the soft, sweatered breasts, blond hair and long, silken legs is holding onto my arm at the Forest Park Highlands bandstand. Kenton's brass is cutting through the lights. My father sees us there. At breakfast the next morning, it's, "Not bad, Jack. She's got legs like a god-damn race horse."

"I wish you wouldn't talk that way," Mom says.

"Great legs are great legs. You should know that."

Mom gets flustered.

On Tuesday night the Rec-Room at school belongs to the upper sophomores. We can bring girls in and there's a little radio room for playing records. We're in the radio room and Mary has just eased herself onto my lap. She adjusts on my thighs like a cat. My erection is almost permanent, and very painful. The night we went to the game in the back seat I couldn't straighten up when we got out. Now she's on it again with her breasts up at my collarbone. Father Michael and a scholastic open the door and stand there. They're only there for a few seconds, but it seems much longer.

Mary is dragging the backs of her nails on my inner thigh. Father Michael's face is bright red. I've seen lust on the face of the church. It's very interesting. They leave without saying a word. That's very unusual.

I've finally reached the point, in my mind, where it's okay to touch her breasts. When I do she twists and her nipples trace my palms. I'm too scared, and too slow, and too god-damned innocent for Mary. She moves on to someone else.

Mary, as I find out, has made it with half the junior class. I
didn't know. At least I got some prestige. I had her on my
arm in public.

My date for the Sophomore Prom is gone but Mom says,
"Oh, I wouldn't worry about that, Jack. Virginia will take
care of that." I'm not sure what she means. What she means
is that Virginia Ascher is running a modeling agency these
days. She can always fix me up with a date. The Saturday
night of the Prom I walk out on the floor with a professional
model in a burgundy evening dress. Her name is Paulette,
and her breasts swell in the gown. She's sweet, too, and kisses
me goodnight.

Socially, my stock has never been higher.

Sometimes Dad goes into an upswing and he gets so he
wants to talk. He's generous. He likes me to sit downstairs
with him and listen to his records. He has stacks. He doesn't
get bitter. He loves good musicians.

"Hey Jack," he yells up the stairs, "I want you to hear
this."

The pills the doctor gave him are dexedrine and phenobar-
bitol. I look them up. I can't follow the technical jargon but
it seems clear that dexedrine keeps you awake and phenobar-
bitol puts you to sleep. I figure it's when he's more on the
dexedrine that he gets enthusiastic. I know he has an open
prescription for both because I'm the one goes to the drug-
store for refills.

Our house operates according to the simple and strict
Code of the Sick Family. Its basic premise is that while yesterday didn't happen, it must never be forgotten.

Monday at breakfast Dad hits me on the side of the head
and chases me out the front door. Tuesday he doesn't come
out of his room. By Thursday he's a solid mass of grief. I sit
with him in his room. Saturday he's jagged and full of author-
ity. Sunday he demands comfort. When Mom doesn't seem

to be able to provide it, she cries for a long time. None of this is out of the ordinary.

I drink every day, and so do most of my friends. I'm not getting anywhere sexually. I missed my chance. I started too high with Mary and now it's time to try again. Going to dances with models is fine but all it contributes to is my image. I'm drunk, horny, and closet-devout.

In the bar it seems better to wait. I wait. King Harrigan is a drinker. He drinks, gambles and passes out. He has rakish good-looks and the kind of off-hand masculinity we all aspire to. He's a diabetic and he's obviously killing himself.

Carol Burke has long, blond hair and cornflower-blue eyes. She follows Harrigan everywhere. If she didn't want Harrigan, she'd seem to be a nice, conventional girl. Her father runs the Burke Iron works. He drinks and plays poker for days. He has ulcers, and they bleed. He's killing himself. I'm the observer at the bar.

My father is big and sick. He doesn't drink any more but he's still killing himself.

I don't know Carol yet, but we're already close. I get to meet her when I help her carry Harrigan to his spotless '46 Plymouth. It's a heavy, clumsy job, and when we finally fold him successfully onto the front seat, she turns and says "Thank you so much," in a breathy voice. Her cheeks are flushed.

In the streetlight and faint neon she's porcelain except for her fanned hair and wet, licked lips. Harrigan is snoring and I'm in love. *Polka Dots and Moonbeams.* Harrigan has plenty of girls. He couldn't care less about Carol. This is common knowledge.

The right word for Carol is haunting. She haunts me. I put in months of phone calls, letters, and reasonably chaste evenings on her front porch. I usually park the old blue Ford a block away from her dark-brick house. I walk up the street slowly and pensively, head down and hands in my pockets.

Sometimes I play poker with her father. When I sit in he gives me a shot and a beer. Sometimes, I don't know why, I feel like laughing at him. Even if I did I don't think he'd notice. He's playing poker. It's his life. I've got one foot in Carol's life. I take her out every night I can.

She's very soft. Her mother is very heavy and very German, but Carol is just soft and slightly confused. She's all I think about. I cut down my bar time. Not my intake. Just the time it takes me to get it down. I write her letters in class. I'm lost.

After a long kiss on her dark porch, the porch is a dim, plum-colored cloister. My face is down in her hair in the shadows where her neck starts.

"I can't, Jack."

I've told her it's time we went steady. Going steady is like announcing you're going to be engaged.

"Why not? We're always together anyway."

"It's just not the way I feel about you."

"I love you."

"I know, but that's not how I feel about you."

I'm off-balance. This isn't how it goes.

"I think we see too much of each other."

Now I can feel the tide moving. I'm losing to Harrigan. Jesus help me.

"Why don't you think about it?"

"I have thought about it and I'm really sorry."

I know there's something to say but I can't think what it is.

"I'm sorry, Jack. I have to go in now."

Back to the bar. I'm an upper senior. Virginia Ascher will have to cover me for the Prom.

"What happened to the little blond?"

Dad just noticed. It's been two months since he threw us all out of the rathskeller. It didn't help me with Carol at all. He stormed in and told me to get the goddamn whores out of the house. Everybody left but Carol. She waited for me while I went up to Dad, drunk, put my arms around his neck and said, "I just want you to love me."

He walked out.

"We broke up two months ago."

"What the hell. What happened to the one with the legs?"

"That was a long time ago."

"C'mon downstairs. I want to talk to you."

He's on an upswing and I'm full of self-pity. He wants to talk about ROTC. I need to take it in college, he knows that, but he also knows that ROTC exists to provide cannon-fodder for the government and he'll be damned if any son of his is going to end up cannon-fodder. It sounds like he might be ready to crack up again. I know he's been worrying about his sister.

"This is how I figure it, Jack. You know I don't want you in music. It's a lousy life. You put years into it and then you wake up one day and you're sitting next to some punk who just got his card and he's making the same money you are. I don't want you in music."

He stops and puts on Benny Goodman's record of *Liza*.

"The way I see it, there's one way you can still fuck the Army. You need to play the tuba, Jack."

His fingers are drumming on the table.

"You sign up for tuba in the band. They always need a tuba in a military band and nobody wants to play the son-of-a-bitch. I'm serious about this and you better be, too. The tuba is your ticket out."

Oh God. He doesn't believe I'm a hero. I know I'm a hero. I'm going to fly planes.

"And for once I don't want any arguments. The tuba is

going to save your goddamn ass, and that's all you need to
know."

No, no, I think not.

Ed and Paul are sitting at the bar.

"What's up for summer," Eddie says.

"I don't know. I have to work."

"The Arcade ain't so bad."

"No."

"What's the matter with you?"

"Nothing."

"Bull-shit."

"What do you think about the tuba, Ed?"

"I don't. I mean, I don't think about the tuba."

Paul leans in.

"What does he want to know?"

"He wants to know what I think about the tuba."

"Jeez. Bad day, huh, Jack?"

The night lights are coming on and I'm never leaving my
stool again.

"What's up with the tuba?"

"Fuck the tuba," I say, "Jesus Christ."

I pull the marks I need to graduate, but not by much.
They don't expect much of me though, and it's okay. Now
I have to take the pre-college exams that all the graduating
Jesuit products take. Without thinking about it, or realizing,
I take them straight. I do as well as I can. I pull grades that
put me in the top two percent of some eight hundred seniors.
My cover is blown.

They call me into the office at school and I'm surrounded
by sad, reproachful eyes. I'd almost like to go back and do
it right.

Dad isn't the only one with plans for me. His are just
the most visible. Mom is planning, hoping, really, for the
priesthood. Johnny at the Arcade, who takes my virginity as

a personal affront, is planning the loss of my innocence. The summer begins and Johnny begins his campaign. It isn't subtle. He buys women and sends them around to service me. Terrible women, sad, burned-out and frightening. They take his money and come to me to earn it.

A knock on the penny arcade shop door brings a woman in a drab, print dress and sneakers. She has a little girl holding her hand.

"Johnny says you want to get sucked off."

I don't deserve this. I really don't think I do.

"Johnny made a mistake. Tell him it went fine."

Toward the middle of the summer I get in the car and head out to Carol's. I've been thinking about her a lot. I make wet circles with my glass on the bar. I tear through the labels on beer bottles with my thumb. It's a beautiful day. I have a pint in the car. Her mother is surprised to see me.

"Carol's out back in the garden. You can just go around if you want to."

She's out on the back steps, just sitting. She's very beautiful in a grey, pleated skirt and pale blue top. She might have posed herself for me.

"I needed to talk to you."

"I'm still sorry, Jack."

I sit down next to her with my arms across my knees.

"I just wanted to explain," I say. "I really got hurt because I'd started to feel like we were always going to be together."

"Well, I couldn't lie to you. What would be the point of that?"

Carol is a very intelligent girl. But she lacks slyness. It's one of the reasons I love her, I think.

"I know that. I mean I didn't come to try and make you change your mind. I just wanted to explain. I didn't feel like you understood me. I just got really carried away and I should have paid more attention to what you were saying. I even went out and bought this."

Resignedly, I reach into my shirt pocket and pull out a gold and diamond engagement ring. I close it up fast in my hand and skim it deep into the goldenrod at the edge of the garden.

"I got carried away is all. I don't blame you and I don't want you to feel bad."

"Oh, Jack."

I stand up and toe the empty milk crate by the steps.

"I just wanted to tell you I understand and I'll see you around if you ever change your mind."

"Jack?"

Back in the car I think about her hunting through the weeds for the ring. She'll never find it and that's to the good. It cost me fifty cents at Woolworth's.

Driving back I don't feel good or bad. I feel at ease. I toast myself with some rye.

"Fuck the tuba," I say out loud.

SEVEN

I keep waiting for God to talk to me. I want so much to know what to do. The sin I can feel inside is deep, and it holds itself in with barbs like a fishhook's. I shouldn't feel this way. It isn't Normal. I believe in the Normal. I don't even know what the sin is, just that it's old and hard. In the place where it's lodged itself, I'll always be five years old.

Nobody knows this but me, and I only know it some of the time.

It's like I'm sorting through the sins the church offers, looking for one that's the image of mine. Some are more important, some less. Stealing and lying are borderline. Much depends on what you steal and why you lie. Drinking isn't a sin at all. But sex outside marriage is. So is masturbation. These are certainties.

I believe in God but it's starting to get obvious that there's something inadequate about belief. I know a lot of people who believe in God, but none of them show me much. I don't find what I'm looking for in them.

The problem is that belief is in my mind and I don't really

trust my mind. At night, if I push my mind as far as it will go, I come flat-up against the wall. When you reach the wall belief doesn't mean anything. There has to be something else.

On a bright, blue day in my green '48 Pontiac, I'm sad and unworldly and priest-ridden and fearful and slick and optimistic and opportunistic and happy. Slightly drunk and glad to be in motion.

I think disconnectedly. There are long spaces between parts of my thoughts like the moving stretches between Burma-Shave signs. I like the way I think. Moving is very important.

I'm a motorized college student on a bright day, and I've had a few beers. I'll be goddamned if I'm going to let the world close in on me. The road is wide open and I'm moving on it. Everything is going to be all right. Drinking *isn't* a sin. It brings me closer to God, like the music.

I manage to slip by the tuba without too much trouble. I take up the bass instead. They're teaching me how to bow it but when I practice I pluck it.

My fraternity is Alpha Delta Gamma—it's the drinker's frat. In my head, Nat King Cole is singing *Too Young.*

"They try to tell us we're too young."

"They tried to sell us egg foo yung," is what Bob comes up with. I don't think it's funny.

Red Sails in the Sunset too, and *Unforgettable.* Woody Herman's *Early Autumn,* with the Stan Getz solo. Getz plays just like I'd like to. He sounds like I feel when I'm sitting in the living room, drunk, and the house is empty.

Sara Vaughan's voice is a very deep armchair.

I plunk the bass.

Calvados will be my drink. Charles Boyer, in *Arch of Triumph,* drinks Calvados. Do Normal people notice what characters in the movies are drinking? Probably not. Charles Boyer and Ingrid Bergman. Ingrid Bergman. I love the darker movies.

Sometimes, when Dad is in one of his upmoods, I haul my bass downstairs and play behind him. He seems to like that, and it's wonderful for me. I try to imagine that the music is bringing us closer together. It isn't, but I pretend. In a very passive, almost drugged-out part of me, I'm looking forward to his death.

His next inspiration, after the tuba, is stenographic school. It's very clear that if I have stenographic skills I'll never end up cannon-fodder. His sudden concern for the wholeness of my limbs is amazing. It seems to be something he broods over.

He doesn't tell me about it first, he just signs me up. I find myself the only male in a beige room full of forty typewriters and thirty-nine aspiring secretaries. I show up two or three times, at night, then fake it. I leave the house as if going, but don't.

Mueller loves the whole idea. For two weeks the whole bar knows me as Our Gal Friday.

My high marks in the entrance exams have got me into a new, and elite, special writing section. There are only sixteen of us, and it's a tough, interdisciplinary grind. I do pretty well, but other things are on my mind. I didn't spend a month working my way into Alpha Gamma Delta so I could spend my nights on assignments. I dunked for raw eggs and crawled two blocks on my hands and knees. I wallowed in pig-slop with blue in my hair and feathers all over me.

Now I want some of the rewards. So I drop out of the writing section and ease back down the ladder.

For my purposes, it's a great fraternity. Mostly we drink. Drunken parties and drunken excursions. We have an identity. We're Alpha Gamma Delta; we career. There's a lot of sex but so much drinking that no one is keeping track of whether I'm getting any or not. That's fine with me.

When the basketball team is heading to Peoria to play Bradley, we all head out too. Compared to Missouri, Illinois is wide open. We don't even go to the game, we go to a strip joint. Not theater-burlesque. It's a bar where the strippers are right in front of you and the revolving glass ball on the ceiling has mirrors in it and throws streams of light across their flesh.

Inevitably, Jack gets sentimental. What kinds of homes did they come from? How did they get here?

A beautiful woman is squatting to pick up a beer bottle with her vagina. Jesus. One of the guys gets her to come to our table. She tells us she can pick up an orange. "You're kidding," we tell her. She says they've got one girl can pick up a grapefruit. We all laugh.

This isn't romantic at all. The romance is in the bourbon. God knows my mother was a dancer, but she never did anything like these girls do. Her dancing is that beautiful picture we have of her on the back fire-escape of some downtown theater. She's in her white, feathery costume, and holding out the sheer part of her skirt with one outstretched arm. Her waist is bare, but it's innocent.

She never had to do anything like this. She wouldn't have done it even if she'd had to. But this woman is beautiful, smart and funny and she's making her living picking up beer bottles with her vagina. This isn't moving me into sex, this is backing me off.

I work in the Med School bookstore and sometimes I go up to the fourth floor where they cut up the Potter's Field bodies. They don't really get them from Potter's Field. They get them before they're sent. It isn't a good thing for me to do, but I can't seem to keep away. Part of my head is always aware of what's going on on the fourth floor.

I finally stop going when I see them open a fat man at the sternum. When the scalpel breaks the tightness of the skin the thick, white sides of the incision roll back from the edge like a kid's idea of how the Red Sea parted. I never want to see anything like that again. My curiosity is gone.

My academic life is non-existent. But I get by. I get by because, for the first time in my life, I find out how to cash in on my sister's perfection. The fact is that a large number of the med-students would like to know her a lot better. She's graduating with a degree in speech therapy, and they've all seen her around. I give them breaks on textbooks, and I make sure they know I'm her brother.

When I'm ready to fail biology I get a rare chance to lift a copy of the test from the teacher's desk. I hustle it down to the cafeteria where three med-students take it for me in about forty-five minutes. They all have the hots for Pat.

"I'm sorry to say that the results of this test were so incredibly poor that I've had to mark it on a curve. I'd also like to say that this is just about the worst showing any class of mine has ever made. My apologies to Mister Erdmann, who had 131 correct answers to the 150 questions."

Mister Erdmann indeed.

I'm becoming more of a mystery every day. There's a luxurious feeling that comes when you see yourself as a spy. I'm not only deep inside myself I'm deep inside them. They don't know it. I imagine I'm growing up.

It's pretty sad.

I pass Physics because of my Carny training. I watch Father Cullen like a hawk. I crack the text for the first time the night before the exam. I've figured out, I think, what he'll ask on the test. There are going to be five essay questions. We'll have to answer four. The night before, I fill four blue books with four essays. I guess right. I pull an A with a commendation.

I've dropped down to a General Studies degree. You can graduate in General Studies, but that's about it. You don't even get in the Yearbook. But that's okay. My vanity is of a different order. I'm a nice guy, a likable guy, and I never get caught.

ROTC is stupid and boring. It's almost important to me because I *know* I'm destined to be a pilot-hero over Korea. In our junior year they take us to an airbase outside Waco, Texas to expose us to the T-33 Trainer. It's a difficult week. Between the hot-shot, sadistic trainer-pilots and the unexpected G-forces, I get pretty sick.

At the end of the week they gather us all in a huge banquet room. There are 800 of us, from schools all over the country. We're the pilots of the future, and we're going to Korea.

Joe Hagerty's already been to Korea and come back. The whole neighborhood turned out for his funeral and there was a lot of whispering about the sealed coffin. Joe had turned out to be a wonderful friend and a genuinely nice guy. I guess my sorrow had a lot of anger in it. Maybe. Mostly I felt confused, his easy face gone into a polished black box with a flag on it.

At night in the banquet room the atmosphere is feverish. The brass are up at a long podium, and flanked by bright new flags. Each college will rise in turn and tell the brass how they feel about what they've seen and done. Mel Thum and I decide that St. Louis University should be different, unique even.

When it's our turn we stand at our table, pull our overseas caps over our eyes, and go into some stand-up comedy. The strange thing is, I start to fly.

I mean I take off on my own, and Mel sits down. A different Jack has elbowed his way out of my head. I can do no wrong. I seem to have an endless supply of stories and one-liners. My voice is manic, and I do impressions. When the crowd laughs too long I put up my hands for silence before hitting them again.

I've never done this before. I don't know where the hell I learned this.

The banquet breaks up and there's a long line of people who want to shake my hand. There's a military wife who lets me know she's *really* impressed. I'm in shock. I let go and somebody else took over.

The question is, who the hell was it?

The extra job at the bookstore is paying off. I'm saving money to go to Europe. I haven't told anyone yet. Between the time I graduate and the time I have to report to the military, I'll have three months in Europe. I'm going to make them sing.

I'm tired of school, I'm tired of home, and I'm tired of hunching my painful blue-balls out of a whole series of back seats. I'm getting the hell out of St. Louis, and I'm getting the hell away from my father. The house too, and the fucking Arcade. Like I said. I'm sad, unworldly, priest-ridden, fearful, slick, optimistic, opportunistic, slightly drunk and occasionally happy.

I wish God would talk to me because I need to hear from someone who knows what's going on. It certainly isn't my father and God seems to be the next one down on the list. At the end of most days I need to sleep in the worst way. I know how. I fall drunk and flat on my bed, sinking into it slowly like a stone in thick, different water.

I've told Pat about my trip. She knows some people in New York. One of them is a writer. His name is Frank Kulla, and he's done some radio work. My ship will leave from New York and even though I'm pretty independent and a good hustler, New York is a little frightening and I need to know somebody.

I break the news to Mom and Dad a week before I'm scheduled to leave.

Mom thinks I should visit Lourdes.

Dad doesn't object, but something strange happens when I tell him. He lapses into complete silence. It depresses him, that's obvious, but it's almost as if the news is so deeply shocking to him that he can't talk. He doesn't say anything. It's something new.

I'm closing out St. Louis as gracefully as I can. I've got myself a flask for traveling. I carry it with me everywhere in my inside jacket pocket. It's thin, silver-plated, and curved just right.

Mom talks to me before I go.

"You've always been a good boy, Jack, I know that."

She's looking straight ahead.

I'm twenty years old.

"The thing we all have to do is to just put our faith in God and take what comes. You know when I heard you playing music with your father I knew that somehow every-thing was going to be all right. It means so much to me, Jack. Now you're off to Europe and I just know things are going to get better. God knows how hard we've all tried, and your father too. There isn't any sickness God can't heal. You must know that."

Grand Central Station is huge and marbled, with high windows arching in a blue haze. It's like my music, it's where I belong. I stay with Pat's friend Frank, just one night, and it's great except for my gut. He takes me to a club to hear Marian McPartland, but my stomach is suddenly kicking in spasms and I can't even hear. He's a nice guy and he gets us a cab to an emergency room. The doctor gives me paregoric. It feels good. Frank's a writer and we sit up late, talking. I tell him the instrument I really love is Gerry Mulligan's baritone.

He laughs and says, "Hey, Jack, let's go. Get yourself a baritone. You gonna wait around or what."

The next morning I'm on the dock at ten. I suddenly feel
like I understand all those songs, the sweet melancholy songs
about New York and autumn. I have a grey sport-coat with
charcoal slacks, a grey, drip-dry shirt, a charcoal grey sweater
and a black raincoat. When we hit a storm I love it. I stand
on deck outside the lounge with my collar up. I'm leaning
casually into the weather.

People buy me drinks. I throw myself into groups with a
genuine desire to please. I feel apart, above, and socially
desirable. The sea is a dream of power. In storms it jumps
up in solid, curved troughs, black, grey and dull green. One
by one, the others get sick. I don't. Alcohol is my gyroscope.
Out by the rail in the wind I wish I had a cape.

In Paris I'm someone else. I'm Gene Kelly. I'm the American in Paris. It's all in my head and that's my safe ground.
I live at the Hotel de Senlis, close to the Sorbonne. For thirty-
five cents a night I get a room, breakfast, and dysentery. I
find out fast that if I drink and don't eat, I can keep it under
control. Wine is fifteen cents a bottle. At night I take off my
grey shirt and wash it out. It drips dry by morning, just like
it says on the label. Masturbation is definitely a sin, but at
night that's hard to remember.

My window opens on a narrow, broken-back street and
the steep, chimnied roofs of old, dreamed buildings. I keep
my bottle of brandy on the window-sill and in the morning
I drink it in sunlight. Bright and beautiful film is being shot.
The exposed reels clutter my table. Flower stalls, little parks
and twilight on the roofs. Paris at night, when the street lights
hit a certain way, old stone is the color of brandy.

My insides are a mess. In cheap restaurants I order a single
potato. Even in cheap restaurants it's embarrassing.

My Michelin map is all marked out. I haven't spent much

money at all and I have two and a half months to go. I've lost ten pounds in two weeks. Without the brandy in the morning, I don't think I could leave the hotel. I start drinking when the sun comes up so I get warm as the air gets warm. Dysentery is a very private problem. I handle it privately. I'm ready to catch a train. "I'm off and running," I think to myself by the window. I laugh out loud, foolishly.

I ride the train and I shoot endless rolls of film of fountains. I used to try to make sure I had a human subject in the foreground. Now it's just the fountains. Fountains and churches and sometimes a long, traveling, underexposed sunset.

I mail my mother a lump of postcards.

I shoot three rolls in the Vatican and buy my family a plenary indulgence. I refill my prescription. Switzerland, Venice, Rome, Naples, Capri, Sorrento, the Italian Riviera, Monte Carlo, Nice and Cannes. At Nice I pick up my forwarded military orders at the American Express. They want me on January 13th. The war is almost over.

In Gibraltar there's a small church down by the waterfront, white stone, like all the old buildings. The rock across the water is massive. I make my confession there to an old Spanish priest. The day is so bright it hurts my eyes. The inside of the church doesn't seem quite so dim as the inside of the average church. I think it's because of the *kind* of light that comes through the colored glass.

"Bless me Father for I have sinned. My last confession was three months ago."

I run it down for him. I've jerked myself off across Europe. I could be brief, but I'm not. Once inside the church I'm struck, as always, with guilt. As if I were right at the top of a stone column of guilty, crumbling Erdmanns.

When I'm finished there's a silence coming out of him.

"My son," he says, "have you thought of giving your life to the church?"

Strangely enough, I haven't.

"This is a remarkable confession. This is the confession of a man who might be a saint."

"Yes, Father."

"Think about your God, my son, and your heart."

"Yes, Father."

He gives me my penances and I wander down the bright street.

Jesus Christ. What have I done now?

He must be used to more significant sins. In a waterfront town, that must be it. I pick up two bottles of scotch for the trip home. My money is almost gone so I'll be going back steerage.

Steerage on the Cristoforo Colombo is vile. The first night I drink enough to get to sleep. In the morning, Sunday, I sneak up to the second-class chapel. By eleven o'clock I'm in the first-class lounge and holding forth to an amused table of monied travelers.

I've taken my medicine, I've had a few drinks, and now I'm a benignly cheerful, adventurous young man who's just come through one of the most whimsical, interesting and anecdotally rich European tours any of them have ever heard about. Sadly, it ends with a trip back in steerage. But that's all right. One takes life as it comes, doesn't one?

I smile winningly.

The Purser comes to tell me in a tight voice that I'll have to return to steerage immediately. One of the women, a naval widow from Baltimore, says no.

"If this young man is traveling in steerage it's not because he belongs there. Are there open cabins in first class?"

"Yes, Madame."

"Well, then, I think you'd better send someone down for his luggage."

"Yes, Madame." The Purser is outraged.

I get to New York first class. I have 10 cents left and a few drops of my prescription. I call Frank and get him at home. He pays for the cab to his place. I weigh a hundred and twenty-nine pounds and each of them is free and drifting. Frank looks at my prescription bottle and laughs, "Jesus, Jack, you got laudanum here."

For the first time in my life, I need to dry out.

EIGHT

The misery twists through the shadowy centers of families like a snake. Generations of the same pain and the same lies. The snake is mechanical, cold clockwork, and never changes direction. Sooner or later someone has to stand aside and say, "No More!" To do it he has to get sober. Dry doesn't make it. Dry is white knuckles and isolate viciousness.

On the last minute of my last roll of film, the clockwork is very clear. Dad is standing on the front lawn. It's cold and he's wearing a hat and a black overcoat. He's holding up a poster I brought him from France and he has a huge, clinically-fixed grin on his face. When the scene changes, Dad has the camera and he's shooting me going up the five front steps.

I'm drooping and sagging theatrically, like an old man, and I go up the steps one at a time and stop with both feet on each landing. My neck is out, and down as far as it will go. It's a first-rate piece of theater. It's a dance of death, and you can probably find something like it in the home movies of any alcoholic family.

Things aren't too bad for the couple of weeks I'm home. It's mostly small talk and some fake enthusiasm. Mom gets me a date with an Ascher Girl. God knows Jack needs to have a good time before he goes off to the Air Force. Her name is Martha Cronkite, and her father is head of psychiatry at the marvelous asylum on Arsenal.

I meet him when I go to pick her up. He's in his den, a small man with a brown moustache and suit. His desk is large and ornate. On the wall to its left is a full-size advertising poster for Marilyn Monroe in *The Seven Year Itch*. She's bent at the waist and the air from a street vent is blowing her skirt up around her thighs. It turns out the good doctor is the president of the local Marilyn Monroe Fan Club. I'd like to kill him. I think of my father, dazed and drooling in his drab little electroshock waiting room, and I watch this little jerk bouncing around like a wind-up toy in his den, and I want to take everything away from him. All his toys. I want to kill him.

"It's been very nice meeting you, Doctor. We won't be very late."

I get a bit too drunk for Ascher Girl sociability. I really have very little to say to her. It isn't her fault. I drop her off on the slick and snowy sidewalk and I don't even walk her to her door. Fuck them both.

The first Air Force stop is Lackland AFB, Texas. Thirty days of indoctrination. Some of the guys make it to the whorehouses. I don't. In my virgin mind VD spreads its rotten bat wings over all the border towns.

Bartow, Florida is where I'll learn to fly. I'm a Lieutenant. Bartow is near Cypress Gardens. I send Mom a postcard of brightly colored girls in hoop skirts at the edge of the swamp.

Our first trainer is a P-18, a modified Piper Cub. We'll stick with it for twenty flight-hours. My instructor is named Bill Miken, and he has an attitude. He's an ex-combat pilot,

WW-II. He knows exactly who we are. We're post-War, ROTC, snot-nosed goddamned fucking fucked-up jerk-off pussies. He doesn't put me at ease.

We go up together in the frightening, open blue, and he screams and rants behind me. *"Fuck* you Erdmann. Fuck you and your whore sister and your whole goddamn pussy family. You'll do this right or I'll tear you a brand new college-boy asshole and you better goddamn well believe I will, you faggoty little prick."

He has his own control stick in back and when he moves it, mine moves too. He slams it back and forth between my knees 'til they're swollen and bruised.

I'm the last guy in the class to solo. I have to solo, and pass, or I'll lose my commission. I don't want to lose my commission. I down a pint and fill my mouth with Clorets.

Miken doesn't seem too bad today. "Okay, Jack, three times. Up, around the field and down."

Sadly enough, I take off without latching the right door. You need two hands to latch it. I can't do it while I'm flying. I'm turning to make my run at a landing and the door flies open. Miken can't see it, it's away from his side. This'll wash me out for sure so I reach out with my right hand and pull it back.

My left hand is on the stick and my right is holding the door shut. To land you have to stall out the engine. I need another hand. I get the stick between my knees and clench them. I'm going to land with my knees. I make it.

That night I drink a fifth of bootleg scotch. It tastes bad, and next day I'm very sick. At the base infirmary they want a urine sample. All I can find is a coke bottle, and when I fill it the piss is so dark it looks like Coke. The nurse in the waiting room asks me if she can have a sip.

"Uh, no, this is my urine."

There's a flurry of activity and I end up in the hospital in

Tampa. The tests come up with nothing, and it goes on my record "kidney and bladder infection due to alcoholic bout." I steal my records and tear that page out before replacing them.

The next plane is the T-6. It's big and blunt-nosed and it lumbers. It looks like it was dropped on the runway. The cockpit has an ominous smell in it. Metal, electricity, leather and sweat.

They've told us anyone can learn to fly. It's not true. I can't learn to fly.

I never know where the horizon is. The T-6 weighs on me. I can tell we're upside down when I can feel my dog-tags in my mouth. That's about it. The intercom is full of screaming.

To land a T-6 you stall it out just before you touch down. You have to come in at a pretty steep angle. When the ground is coming up at me I pull back too soon on the stick and stall out thirty feet over the runway. All that metal comes down on its wheels and struts and we bounce twenty feet up. The next time it's ten. I start to use the rudders and brakes and go into a ground loop. An ambulance is screaming down on us from my left. There are fire trucks waiting. I stop in the grass off the runway.

I don't need this. I go out of my way to fuck up everything I touch, hoping to wash out. I let the instructor see me trying to take off the gas cap by turning it the wrong way. Finally, the instructor's had enough. It's after I've almost landed cockpit down. We're out on the runway.

"Erdmann," he says, "get your ass off this field. Take your goddamn parachute and get the hell off the field and don't ever come fucking back again."

It's okay.

I lightly head for the Officer's Club. One of the nice things about being an alcoholic in the military is that you rarely have to pay for your liquor. The other is that you don't stand out. In the Air Force even nonalcoholics drink alcoholically. There isn't much else to do. It's an alcoholic convention. They should issue us paper party hats.

I never have to fly again and life is going to be all right. In a rare burst of demonstrative humor, the Air Force sends me to Salina, Kansas. I pass through a dust storm outside Topeka. I have to keep the windows shut and the temperature is pushing 100. No pine trees, no lakes, no mountains, no brocade. The dust on my eyebrows looks like makeup.

At Smoky Hill AFB (there's no hill) Father Joe is, for now, my one positive encounter. Alcoholically positive. He drinks as much as I do and we sit in his bare room (no crucifix) and drink Old Crow and play cribbage in the heat. He tells me a lot about himself. About Chicago, about his doubtful vocation, about the Major's wife he's in love with. I serve mass for him.

I'm back again with Harry Book and Father Malachi's bleary, angry eyes. I don't seem to have come very far. The difference now is the priest isn't just a drunk. He's also in love with a woman. Out of a hundred games of cribbage he beats me ninety-six times. When he wins he giggles in the back of his throat. When we're both real drunk and hot on a Sunday afternoon, he goes to his dresser and comes back with a photo he confiscated from an enlisted man. It's antique porn. A pretty, plumpish girl is sitting naked in a heavy armchair. Standing next to her is a naked man, and she's holding his erection in her left hand.

"What have I done with my life, Jack? It looks like I missed out."

His eyes are bright and he looks at the picture and giggles.

"Looks all right to me," he says.

Smoky Hill is a SAC base. Sometimes in the very early morning we have emergency drills. So I'm out drunk on the field at dawn supervising the loading of A-bombs into the bays of B-47's. There's only about a quarter inch clearance all the way around, but in the morning, when I'm drunk, I feel cold and competent. This is a very strange life.

I feel like we're extras on a set. I meet Jake Carson in the Officer's Club. He's a jazz fan, and we talk. He lives in a basement apartment in town. The walls are cement and his brass double bed sits in the old coal bin. All the light comes from 25-watt red bulbs. The windows are taped over. One of the walls is nothing but photographs, pictures of every woman he's had in Salina. They're pornographic action shots. Their one constant is that Jake's head has been cropped out. There's one of the wife of a previous base commander. She's perched on the edge of a bed wearing nothing but a string of pearls. A coke bottle is halfway up her vagina and she's holding it delicately, with two fingers. Jake is a sinister guy. Eddie Morris, my base roommate, says Jake would fuck a woodpile on the chance there'd be a snake in it.

I don't tell Father Joe about Jake. These are different worlds. I'm certain from the day I get involved with Jake that my virginity is almost at an end. So be it. He lives in a half-world of hipness and vice. Vice is precisely the right word. He could be carny. He picks up on people's secret openings and moves in. He wants me to take pictures for him. He's currently making it with the wife of an Airman in his crew, and he wants me over Saturday morning to photograph them. My need to be cool is much too great for me to turn him down. So is my curiosity and I show up, showered and shiny, at ten Saturday morning.

He yells through the door to come in.

Inside, Jake is lying on his back and the woman has just the tip of his cock in her mouth. She's kneeling on the bed between his legs in nothing but an open man's shirt, and both her hands are flat on his chest. She's quite lovely. I can't breathe.

"Hey Jack, the camera's on the dresser. It's all set."

She's taking his cock farther into her mouth in little, very slow nibbles. Her eyes flick out at me from the side through fairly long, brown hair. I take the pictures but I feel like I'm betraying something.

"How about this, Jack? Look good?"

He's got her leaning over the table facing me and he's standing behind her with his hands on her hips.

"Don't get my head."

Her name is Lila and she's looking at me. She gasps and drops her head so her hair falls in front. When she looks up again she smiles and licks her lips at me. On her way out she drags her hand across my belly.

"Thanks, Jack. Maybe we could have a couple of drinks sometime."

"Sure."

"How about tomorrow?"

"I'll call you."

She closes the door behind her.

"Goddamn," Jake says, "she loves it."

On the phonograph Carmen McRae is singing *When Sunny Gets Blue.*

Lila lives in a very small frame house. She brushes my cheek with a kiss at the door.

She's not really interested in the drinks. But I've taken care of that in the car on the way over. Sitting on the couch with Lila, a drink in my hand and the light faint through one of those heavy lampshades, yellow with thick purple fringe, my heart is stepping down to a detached resolve. With alcohol things happen to you. You watch and endure.

I have a brief flurry of terror in the bedroom, but Lila is so much everywhere, so much sliding, soft power that with almost no awkwardness I'm out of my clothes and onto the bed. I'm sure I won't be able to perform. It's a matter of some fatality. From my observer's stance I know I'll live through it. Lila twists and sighs and drags her nails lightly in the small of my back. We haven't spoken more than three or four sentences since I got here.

"Oh, God, That Feels Good," she says.

Suddenly I understand. I'm a foot from her belly with no erection and no chance of getting one and she's going into her ecstasy mode. It's in her head. It doesn't matter how many lovers like Carson she's had. It doesn't matter that I'm the Virgin Prince. It's okay and I'm ready. With her help I push into her smoothly and she raises her belly to meet me in a solid stop. We stay in the bed for two or three hours, jumbled and wet all over.

I don't know it, but the baby's crib is in the corner by the window and the baby is sleeping in it. The last time we come together noisily, he wakes up and starts to cry. I can see him in the street-light, hanging off the edge of the crib and crying.

I don't know quite who I am anymore. It isn't just the mortal sin that bothers me, though God knows this is mortal sin with a vengeance. It's more that I never wanted this. I wanted the sex, and the sex was wonderful, but I didn't want a married woman and I didn't want to make a child cry at his mother's screams in the dark. It's not like I ever really did know who I was. What I had was a house-of-cards personality that relied equally on who I wanted to be, who I thought I was, and who I thought other people thought I was.

I always thought I had an honorable core. Shaky, maybe, but not a hypocrite. My moods come and go but the liquor stays. I pay hard dues for my secret life. That's what tells me I'm not a hypocrite. Events break my heart. I level out the pain with booze but I pay, don't I?

Lila had red, dark panties on. She said she wore them just

for me. We did things you're not supposed to do. I'll make
my confession to Father Joe. It'll be embarrassing, but safe.
I don't expect him to be too stern about sex with a married
woman. He loves one too.

I'm right. "Well, I suppose it had to happen, Jack. You've
got to try not to let it happen again."

The base is full of predatory married women and I'm a
newly-non-virginal drunk.

"Yes, Father."

I hang out at Jake's place. We listen to jazz and get drunk.
He has a beautiful, rainy photograph of 52nd Street in Man-
hattan. It's *the* jazz street. Steam is coming out of the openings
in manhole covers and the jazz clubs recede down the length
of the street. It's a wonderful picture. It's framed on a wall
by itself.

When Colonel Wilson gives me the job of revamping the
base educational program I hustle, weasel, bully and slip
regulations. When I'm finished we receive a citation for having
the best educational stats in the country. They take my picture
for the Air Force paper.

I make my Colonel feel secure, and he likes that.

He makes me Officer-in-Charge of the Airmen's Club and
Air Force Band Commander. My men love me. I put a cocktail lounge in the Day Room for them. This is not regulation.

I'm not seeing Lila anymore but there are plenty of women
in town and at the Officer's Club. Lila is not what you would
call a solid, sweet home-body. I'd never marry Lila. I have
my standards. Romance as light as *Singin' in the Rain;* sensual-
ity as deep as *Notorious;* day-to-day life as solid and flowing
as *Meet Me In St. Louis.*

I'm looking around for the woman. She'll have to be a
drinker too. I don't really know that, but it's a fact. My future
is laid out in my head in images. It has all the reality I'm
capable of. The first thing I notice about Sara is how comfort-

ably she laughs. She's sitting at the bar and her laugh comes through the noise, warm and sexy. She drinks like I do. I can see that right away. She's perfect.

I take her out but I never press her for sex. This, after all, is the future mother of my children. I can come by sex in other places. Why cheapen my images? I haven't told Sara she's the future mother of my children yet, but I'm sure she knows. I know she'll agree. She wants out of Salina in the worst way.

I start to spend a lot of time at her house with her parents. With her mother, really, her father can't move. He's had a stroke and all he can do is sit in the big chair in the parlor.

It's a big, solid house, with white entrance columns and tended landscaping. Sara's mother drinks more than Sara. The bar is always open. Father Joe likes to come with me on my visits. He comes for the liquor, and because of his loneliness. I like him to come. It does a lot for my image to come calling with a priest.

Sara has a teenaged brother. He's pretty friendly and I like him. We're all smashed in the parlor the night his father has another stroke in his chair. It kills him and when it's clear he's dead, the boy laughs. I recognize the sound and I'm terribly embarrassed. Everyone covers up fast, and Father Joe suddenly becomes clerical.

Jack Erdmann has become a hero to the women of the Carlin family. He brought a priest with him the night Daddy died. With manners like me I'd be an ornament to *any* family.

I get myself a '28 Chrysler touring car with tasseled curtains and velvet seats. I find it in a farmer's barn and he lets me have it for $25. The Eldorados and the Lincolns get stuck in the Kansas winter, but not me.

Collom makes me Casualty Assistance Officer. This is the worst of my Air Force life. I have twelve duties and one of them is notifying the next of kin when an Airman's been killed. I go to the crash sites, too.

When I've done everything I'm supposed to, Father Joe and I look up the dead man's file to find out his religion. Most of the families I see live in houses like I'm in. There are lots of kids. One woman looks at me and without moving her face at all says, "He got up late and he couldn't eat. I gave him a cheese sandwich." Her kids are out in the yard.

On Sundays I go with the Carlin family out to the Brookville Hotel. We have a marvelous Sunday dinner of fried chicken and buttermilk biscuits. Sara is great. She *cares* about me and I'm deeply touched. I have to marry Sara. Another one who cares might never come along.

The way Sara is I can do what I want and she'll always be there. My drinking doesn't bother her. It seems like the only thing that bothers her is Salina. Our arrangements have become formal. We'll be married as soon as I'm out. I'm twenty-four with six months to go.

I'm going to be a lawyer and Sara is going to be waiting for me when I get home and the kids are going to be sweet and loved. I'll never be anything like George. I don't get nasty when I drink. That's not the only difference. I couldn't stand to hurt a child. They get so confused when they're hurt. It would kill me to hurt my own child.

After dinner, when the kids are asleep, I'll sit in my big chair with a glass of good brandy.

NINE

I'm in the pay phone outside the second floor bar of the whorehouse in London at 105 Gloucester Place West. The bar is all red, deep-red velvet, and the halls are wood-paneled. Captain Thiebaud has just gone by chasing a giggling girl in an Air Force shirt. In the soft light the cheeks of her ass are peach-colored. I've been here for three days.

"Hello, Dot?"

"Oh, hello, Jack."

"I don't have much time, this is a pay phone. I want to ask you for Sara's hand in marriage."

"Well, Jack, that's the sweetest thing I ever heard. Of course you can marry Sara. It would make me very happy if you did. I'm sure you know that."

"That's great. Tell Sara, I have to go."

"Take care now, Jack."

I go back to Monica. Monica is wonderful. She's my height and so controlled, so self-absorbed in bed that it feels like she's milking me. When she's on top it's exactly like she's milking me. She pulls from inside her belly and her muscles stretch and relax in the same long action. When I'm ready to come she leans forward and covers my mouth with hers like she wants to catch my breath at the moment. It's like nothing I've ever felt. I'm so relaxed I don't recognize myself.

These are the memories I'm going to take back to Kansas. Right now, that seems okay. On the plane, it doesn't anymore. I look across the way at Jake Carson. Jake doesn't live like a real man. Jake, in fact, is damned from here to eternity. I haven't thought about damnation for quite a while. but it's still there. It clicks in just like always.

I wonder where Bob Mueller is these days. And Paul Meiners. It was warm in the Savoy, and we liked each other. The third bottle from the left on the second shelf up is Chartreuse. I wonder if Carol is still hanging around. Harrigan had some dignity. He knew what he was doing, anyway.

December 27th there are a thousand people in Sacred Heart, the biggest Catholic church in Kansas. I know about thirty of them. I'm in the Sacristy in my tuxedo. My chest is clenched and I'm not sure what the matter is. I do know what the matter is. I think I'm making a mistake. I more than think it. I feel it. I'm physically sick. I want this crap over with, the reception too. When it's all over we're heading to New Orleans for our honeymoon. New Orleans should be as romantic as you can get.

We're going to New Orleans in my Chrysler. That's perfect. Before we leave I lift two cases of wine for the trip. I've had to stand for three solid hours shaking stranger's hands at the goddamn Salina Country Club. With nothing to drink. My system feels it. I'm continually glancing at Sara to reassure myself that yes, she's an attractive, sexy lady who loves me and everything, thus, will be fine once I get out of this stinking line and we get out on the road where I can stop somewhere for a few drinks, for both of us, and feel free, open and ready for the world. I like the way her breasts swell in the white silk. I think sex without sin is going to be great. I've already confessed to the other stuff.

We stop somewhere the first night, Texas, Oklahoma, I don't know. The desk clerk at the motel offers us the bridal suite. I've got rice in my hair. The night is a wavering, drunken mist. Maybe we have sex, maybe we don't. Who knows. The night is mainly exhaustion and enough alcohol to fill an aquarium.

When we get to New Orleans I tell Sara to put her head down. I don't want her to see anything before we get to the French Quarter. The city itself is not going to be allowed to sully Sara's perception of New Orleans, nor of me.

We go to a lovely, small hotel called the Maison de Ville. It's pure French Quarter, with a courtyard filled with semi-tropical lace. There's a stone fountain, and the shutters facing the courtyard are old, green wood on the salmon stucco. It's perfectly lovely and the courtyard has a gate that opens into the bar at The Court of the Two Sisters. I have to make two trips from the car to the room. One with the luggage and one with the case of Old Crow I picked up en route. It seemed the sensible, economic thing to do.

We have dinner at Antoine's. Sara's in a black evening dress and her face is prettily flushed. She holds my arm and rests the side of her face on it.

Our room is dimly lit and thick with atmosphere. We get ready for bed by the book, Sara off in the bathroom with her suitcase, and me on the bed in new, light pajamas. When she comes out I fly into a rage. Not a visible rage, but a churning interior anger that stops right below my throat like a lump of scream.

She's standing between the bed and the light and her hands are on her hips in a three-quarter pose. She's got on high heels, black-silk stockings and a garter belt. This isn't Sara. She's dressed and trying to act like a goddamn whore, and

I hate it. She's fucking with my images. And she doesn't look right that way, she's not doing it right. What am I supposed to do? Grunt and throw her on the bed? This is my virgin princess—she's too goddamn dumb to know it.

It's the angriest I've every been. I want so much to believe in the life I imagine. Sara is blurring the outlines and I feel like I've been trapped in a small space where reality isn't what I want it to be but just the simple accumulation of twenty-five years of grinding, little-boy fear.

She comes to bed but she sees I'm not smiling. I don't know what my face looks like, but I can guess. Sara can see it. She must. I take her in a rage and our marriage has its formal beginning. When it's over there's a look on her face like she's stuck in a dream that's just beginning to get threatening. The faces have started not to look right. But we go to sleep. I get up around three-thirty and pour myself a healthy drink in the bathroom.

We do everything there is to do. The track, the Sugar Bowl for football, jazz most every night. We manage to bring off New Year's Eve. It's not quite right, but who's to say so?

Sara dresses carelessly, she's almost frowsy. She dresses like she thinks she's an ugly duckling. She isn't. I hate myself for being embarrassed when she doesn't look right. I could tell her she's not an ugly duckling but I think it would hurt her.

New Year's Eve we're in O'Brien's for the jazz. The house photographer takes our picture. It's a photograph I'll look at often. Sara is leaning forward in mid-sentence and she looks a bit earnestly drunk. I'm looking at the camera with a very sickly, very squishy grin on my face. I'm wearing a paper hat, askew, and I'm a lot drunker than Sara. There's an implicit apology in the grin and my eyes are scared.

Apology to who?

Scared of what?

It must be in New Orleans that Sara gets pregnant. We both want children, so that's okay. We both see children in our futures the way a developer might see a building on a vacant lot. We have loose ends to tie up in Salina. Sara has to finish school. Marymount College. I work in a clothing store and wait. Every night, after dinner, we kill a bottle of B&B. Why B&B? I don't know. I don't even like it.

Sara graduates, and we head to Denver. I'm enrolled in the University of Denver Law School. The day we leave is the day Sara finally gets out of Salina for good. She's very happy. Denver isn't Paris, but neither is it Salina. I'm a little sad to go. Father Joe and Jake have been the kind of friends I'm at ease with, and I love them for it. I'm not at ease very often. Jack's life is a railroad, though; sometimes I get to hang around a station waiting to change trains. I still like that. I haven't found out yet what kind of train it is.

I have some romantic notions about Criminal Law.

Our new apartment is in Golden, Colorado, on the out-skirts of town not far from the Coors Brewery. Our building is on a flat, red, ugly, empty road. The world is mostly sky. I drive six or seven miles to school every day through sky and red dirt. It gives me time to think, and I need it. I'm making my big push for the good life. Law School is going to go the way I want it to. Law School is my first clear shot at showing what I can do.

Sara is pregnant with Steve and stuck in the middle of nowhere. There's always plenty of beer because our neighbor Hal is an assistant brewmeister and brings Sara a case every afternoon. Her pregnancy shows, sixth months or so, with rosiness and sometimes deep calm. Hal is usually there when I get home. He hangs around with Sara and drinks. It gets to be usual for me to come home and find Sara giggling on Hal's lap in the big chair. They like to listen to the sound track from *The Music Man*.

I treat Sara with considerable lightness, especially when someone else is around. I go into my banter mode. I usually start with a priggish, morally earnest face. I keep my eyes blank but I can shift them into a leer with a minimum of adjustment. I float a couple of inches above the conversation. I'm good with my shoulders and hands and my impersonations are very dry. I live by the non-sequitur and change my persona every two minutes. Sara loves it.

When we're alone, things are different. I get morose easily. I imagine that's just the way married people are. I don't talk a lot, but what's to talk about? The brewmeister means nothing to me. I'm working hard. I really don't think there's anything between them. If he's in love, he's in love. It gets us free beer. I really am working hard. We go to the movies a lot.

"*The Music Man,* well, I'll be damned. Now I think that's the way music should sound, don't you, I mean really. Jazz, drugs and Coors. That's the trouble with this goddamn country and if it comes down to it, I'll stick with barbershops and high-school marching bands and I don't give a damn who knows it, that's the kind of guy I am, wouldn't you say, dear?"

"The beer is in the fridge."

"Now that's what I mean about the homely virtues. Things have their place and they're in it."

She stands up and follows me into the kitchen to kiss my cheek.

"How was it today?"

"Pretty good. I'm in the running for the Judge Crater Civics Award."

"Uh huh. I didn't start dinner. I thought maybe we could eat out and go to the movies."

"Fine with me. Hal coming?"

"No, he's going home."

Hal is still sprawled half-down in the chair. He's a big

man, with an angular, western face. He's moving his lips to *Till There Was You*. I'm reasonably sure nothing is going on. Who has an affair with a pregnant woman? And we've only been married six months. Sara isn't like that. I think about it anyway. I decide I really don't have the time to care. I don't know how I got so cold so fast. Hell, I'm not cold, I'm just realistic. The new Jack is going to need to be realistic.

"Want to catch a movie with us. Triple bill, 75 cents."

"Nah, I gotta get home."

"Your trouble is you let life pass you by. Triple bills in this kind of company don't turn up every day. When was the last time you got to see a triple bill with Clarence Darrow and his Belgian mistress?"

He laughs a little.

"No thanks, not tonight."

Movies or not, I'm going to be up late studying Real Property Law. What I'm doing is memorizing the Hornbook. Hornbooks are complete texts on the nature and applications of specific laws. I'm memorizing Moynihan on Real Property.

Real Property is a bitch of a course. I'm scared of the final, but once I memorize Moynihan everything is going to be fine. The night before the final I sit upstairs and sweat every word of Moynihan into my head for the last time. Downstairs Hal and Sara sound like they're into their second case of beer. They're singing along with *Gary, Indiana*.

In the morning I'm still reading Moynihan and Sara is passed out on the couch. I don't know when Hal went home. I feel good. I'm just at the right level of hallucination for the information to be at my fingertips. The best test in a given class is graded A-1. There's only one to a class, and it's me. Overall, I'm solidly in the top half of my class. Maybe I don't feel as good about it as I might, but I'm used to that. I've never felt really good about anything I've done. But all I really need is to get the job done. People will think I feel good. It's almost the same thing.

I don't drive the Chrysler any more. Now I have a Daimler-Benz. It's dark green, it has wheel wells and a wooden steering wheel. It has a five-speed transmission and a sun roof. It's a '39. It barely runs but it only costs me $800.

Sara and I aren't getting much closer. We keep the house filled with friends and liquor so we don't have to notice. We drink to separate drummers.

Steve is born in October 1959. Sara wakes me in the middle of the night and we make the ride to Denver, barely.

I've seen movies of expectant fathers so I know what to do. I pace and I smoke. I'm Dagwood Bumstead. Sara delivers in half an hour. He's a beautiful baby. I guess all first babies are uniquely beautiful. It strikes me that he looks a lot more human than I'd expected. That night I sneak up to her room with a bottle of Mumm's and two glasses. The forms of romance are very important to me.

Three months later, my college career comes to an end.

"Hello, Jack?"

"Yes, Mom."

"How's everything and the baby and all."

"Just great, Mom. He sleeps a lot more now. I'm not so tired all the time."

"That's wonderful, Jack, but the reason I called is things aren't too good here and I don't like to bother you with it, I know how busy you are, but I'm just not strong enough for all of this and I don't know where else to turn, Jack."

"What's the problem, Mom?"

"Well, it's your father, Jack. He's back in the hospital again for those treatments and I guess that's all right, I guess they'll work again, but the problem is the Arcade, Jack, and I just don't know what I can do. The doctor says he's going to be in there a lot longer this time, six weeks maybe, and when he gets out he's not much use for a while and I just can't handle it there, all that time by myself. I just don't think I can, Jack, and you know it's all we have. You know that."

"I don't know what I . . ."

"If you could just come back for a while. Just till everything's all right again. You know Dad would never ask you. He doesn't even know I'm doing this and I don't want to give him any more to worry about. Last time I went in he didn't even know me, Jack. It was so awful he didn't know me and his eyes didn't move, like I wasn't even there."

She's crying now.

"I'll be there, Mom. Everything's going to be okay. You hear me? Stop crying now. We'll all be back and everything will be okay. You'll love the baby. Now you don't worry about it, and I'll call you tomorrow and let you know when we're getting in."

I sit down on the balcony. First I put on my big coat. I sit there and knock back a fifth of cheap gin. It must be three in the morning when I get to bed. Sara isn't going to like this.

"But what about school?"

"It's just for a little while. There are law schools in St. Louis. I can transfer."

"Do you really think it won't be for very long?"

"Jesus, Sara, I really don't know. I don't have any goddamn choice."

"What about Pat?"

"Pat's husband has a legal practice already. They're not going to pack up and move in with Mom."

"I guess not."

"It'll be fine. Seeing the baby will cheer her up."

"I don't like the way you look."

"Jesus, Sara."

"Well, I don't. You look like your stomach hurts. Your mouth looks different."

"Well, fuck it, Sara, my stomach does hurt, okay? I'm doing the best I can. You want a drink?"

"Sure."

"You and Steve can go by train Saturday. I'm driving."

"Driving? You'll never make it."

"It'll be fine."

I drive them to the train station. Hal the brewmeister waves goodbye from the middle of the road.

Sunday I pack up the car. Monday morning I hit the road.

Driving is good for me. I don't go fast because I can't, and I have that nice disconnected feeling I get by myself in a car. I have bourbon and gin, and the heater works.

I eat in sleazy diners and I sleep in sleazy motels. I never get really drunk. I maintain myself the way I like to think I'm maintaining the car. Wide, flat, and sometimes snowy horizons to head into in a warm bubble of car. I don't care what the engine is like. I just want to turn up on Winona St. in a Daimler-Benz.

In my head, St. Louis looks dark and metallic. It sits on the map like a dark metallic drain and I'm moving at the outer edges of the swirl. A swirl with buildings. Clumps of trees and bar lights. The Mississippi. Winona St. has one of those little, red enamel dots on it. "You Are Here."

I'm outside Kansas City when the car goes. The sound of a thrown rod. I roll off the road and sit there. The clouds are high and dark. It isn't raining hard yet, but it will. You can tell. The drops are large and they splash hard on the windshield.

I get out the couple of small cases I'm going to need and slam the trunk. It bounces up and I slam it again with the side of my fist. I kick out the left taillight.

I stand my cases neatly by my side and stick out my thumb in the rain. "Motherfucking son-of-a-cocksucking-bitch."

T E N

Winona St. is a row of wet trees. The dark, wet brick has the coldness of real stone but inside the houses it's warm. That's the way it's supposed to be. I feel like the cold comes in with me.

The first thing I do is to go to the hospital, the asylum, whatever. Dad looks right through me. He's a lot fatter and he's in a bed that looks too small. The big sleeves on his blue pajamas are hanging off its sides. There isn't much point in saying anything.

"Doctor Ullman?"

"Yes."

"I'm Jack Erdmann, George Erdmann's son."

"Ah yes, Mr. Erdmann, what can I do for you?"

"Well, I'd like to know about my father."

"In what sense?"

"What's wrong with him, what you're doing about it, whatever you can tell me."

"Your father's a very sick man, Mr. Erdmann."

"No shit."

"Pardon me?"

"What do the shock treatments do? I mean why shock treatments? What are they doing?"

"Experience tells us that in cases of chronic and incapacitating depression, that electro-shock therapy produces the most immediate and most reliable relief."

"I understand that. What I want to know is what they're doing. When do we reach the point where he doesn't come back?"

"Well, if you'll forgive me, Mr. Erdmann, I think you're indulging a bit in a layman's taste for the dramatic. Individual reactions are a function of the pathology of the individual disease. I think you can rest assured that we're quite skilled at what we do."

"What disease?"

"I wish we could give you some cut-and-dried answers on that but the fact is, mental illness is not a cut-and-dried affair. The best we can do right now is assure you that your father can lead a reasonably stable life."

"Yeah. I just saw him. He's pretty stable."

"I don't know that sarcasm is appropriate to the situation. I think for your own sake, and certainly for your mother's, that you should make some effort to come to terms with the reality of your father's needs. I wouldn't say that your coming here intoxicated is of any real help to anyone."

"I know the realities. My father came in here a drunk. Now he's a vegetable."

"Alcoholism is a symptom, Mr. Erdmann."

"How about drug addiction?"

"I think we're talking at cross purposes."

"That's probably true."

"If you'll excuse me."

"Kiss my ass."

Mom explains it to me.

"It's just like he runs down. When I go to see him he's not too bad but a little dazed, then he sits around for a couple of days as nice as he can be and then he's George again and he does the things he has to and everything's all right. I can always tell though. He starts to ask me questions I can't answer. About anything at all but mostly dying and what happens, and being alone, and his sister of course, and then I know he'll be back in his room soon and crying. It took six months last time. You'd think with all the pills he's supposed to take that something would work. With the shock it's better than it would be, I would have to say that, Jack, it's better than it would be."

Sara is sitting in Dad's big armchair. She has the fixed, bright look she gets when she's concentrating on not being drunk. "When Daddy had his stroke we had to get used to him just sitting there. Sometimes we forgot he was there he was so quiet."

"Well, I thank God every day Jack found you, Sara. I'd get so afraid you know, you get so afraid for your children but Pat is just fine and very happy with Karl and now Jack has found you. I really don't have much to complain about it's just that I get the feeling sometimes that George might not know me anymore and die that way and I couldn't stand that, I really couldn't."

"I think we could use another drink. It's too early in the year to be depressed. Mom?"

"Thank you, Jack, I think I could have another. What do you call these now, giblets?"

"Gimlets, Mom, gimlets."

"Jack and George used to have such terrible fights, Sara. But Jack would always try to make it right and he always tried to stay as cheerful as he could when things were bad. He was just a little boy and he'd sit with his father for hours and tell him such beautiful things about faith and the Church and the way the Virgin cares for us. It made me very proud and I couldn't do it because he'd make me cry. Oh, there you are, Jack. Tell Sara what the sisters told you when you went out to the convent for those painting lessons or something."

"I don't remember, Mom. It's a long time ago."

"Well, whatever. They were *so* impressed with Jack and they thought he might have a vocation, didn't they, Jack?"

"I think so."

"I can't say I thought very much of some of the girls he brought to the house but when I met you Sara, and I watched you in the Church I knew everything was going to be all right."

"Thank you, Marian. Everything is all right."

Mom is beaming.

"I want you to know that this is your home. Don't bother about me, you do whatever you have to do to make yourself comfortable. It's so nice to have a baby in the house again."

"He's beautiful isn't he."

The Savoy is still open. I go all the time and it makes me feel sad in the nice, pillowy way. The past is all around me like a hero's cape.

The park is empty and dreamlike and the Arcade is dark. When I turn on the power at the box, the lights throw the hall into the pronounced emptiness of a morning-after. I look around for a little while but I can't find a damn thing to do. The jobs are there but I just can't see them. I turn off the lights and drift out. Black raincoat, collar up, self-conscious melancholy. I'm not sure I really feel things. Sometimes I feel like I just woke up on a stage.

Every night I look in on Steve in his crib. How do I protect him? All I can see is his little turned head. I need to know I can protect him.

I'm starting to get used to that hollow feeling that opens

in a parent's chest. I'm not really getting used to it, but I'm coming to expect it. I look around the room for a long time. It's like I'm looking for something but my eyes stop at random and stay without seeing. Nobody knows who I am, and that's a fact. That's my strength. If I keep it, I'll be all right. Lead from your strength. You have something tiny to protect. If you fail, you're not going to want to be alive.

Dad comes home in early July. He's pleasant enough but there are big gaps in his memory. He walks very slowly, with little steps, and when he's not in his room, he's downstairs eating. He doesn't play, not even a little. He makes the right noises at Steve, but there isn't any recognition there.

We need to get away. "It's okay, Mom, it's just things are a little confused right now. Too much to do, not enough time. Sara's pregnant again."

"Oh, why didn't you tell me before. That's wonderful, Jack. Right now I think it's the best news you could have given me."

"We just found out."

"Maybe this one will be a girl, Jack. Do you think so?"

"Maybe, Mom, I really couldn't say."

"And you know we're always here for anything you need."

"I know, Mom."

"What do you think about doing now, now that you're not in school?"

"I'm a pretty good salesman."

She laughs.

"Well, that's certainly true. You could always talk me out of anything."

If the sales professions didn't exist, the skid-row population would double overnight. I get started in mutual funds.

David is born in June. He's a beautiful baby. I go down to the Savoy to celebrate by myself. I don't want to go to

Winona St. The last time I was there I walked in without knocking and I could hear Dad yelling in the kitchen.

"Son-of-a-bitch you goddamn whore. You don't give a goddamn what happens to me as long as you get the money and your stuck-up bitch mother is happy. I could die on the floor and you'd both goddamn step over me. I can't stand it, Marian. You don't know how I goddamn feel. You don't even care with your goddamn whoring church. You don't even goddamn care."

Dad is back.

"I know what I said, Jack, but sometimes it's true. Sometimes he stays all right for a while after the hospital, but when he gets like this I don't know what to do because it's always the same and soon he'll be crying and I'll have to sit and hold him again. I wish our lives had been different, Jack."

It's okay that things aren't different at the Savoy. By now I know most of the guys at the bar.

Lou the bartender buys me a drink at the Savoy.

"When are you packing up?" he asks me.

"Two weeks."

"What's the big deal in California?"

"I met this woman in Europe and she told me about a town called Sausalito. Sounds really beautiful. She made it sound like heaven."

"A woman in Europe. I don't suppose she lives in Sausalito now, huh? You wouldn't pack up your wife and kids to California just to get a little on the side?"

"I'm not like that, Lou. You've hurt me deeply."

"And I don't suppose you got in her European pants, huh?"

"Really, Lou."

"I'm going to miss you, Jack. You're a helluva guy."

When I leave, I drive by Winona St. but the lights are all out. In the dark it's a toy street in the moonlight. I never should have come back here but what the hell else could I do? I wish my father would die. It's very clear to me in the dark and white street. There's nothing to feel bad about. He'd be better off dead and Mom deserves better. And maybe with him dead, I'd feel better too. Maybe to be a free man your father needs to be dead. Maybe that's true for everyone. People don't talk about their real feelings. Nobody's straight about stuff like that. I can't be the only one.

I have a half pint in the glove compartment. It's my California car, a brand new 1938 Buick Century. It's nice to sit alone in my past and drink. I like the scale. I feel like I'm going to be free.

It's hard to believe. The morning we're leaving I go out to the car with a suitcase and the hood is gone. Somebody came by in the night and stole the hood off a goddamn '38 Buick. I'm very quiet. I go to the Arcade and lift a tarpaulin. I tuck it over and around the engine. It's going to have to do.

I pull a seven-by-fourteen trailer with four rooms of furniture in it. Mom and Dad wave goodbye from the curb. Sara's sister lives in Malibu, and when we get there I unhook the trailer and drop off the family. I'll go to San Francisco first and rent us a place. In Sausalito.

I love driving up the coast by myself. In San Francisco I only stop for a couple of drinks and directions. The Golden Gate is perfectly beautiful. It's a bright, clear day and its lines are electric red, and etched. The Pacific is on the left through a bellied, soft-hill opening.

I don't need any convincing about Sausalito. I come down a long, winding hill onto a street that fronts the bay like a soft belt. It's a dream town. It curves around the bay in a little concave belly, and the houses back up the deep hill in steep, hidden steps.

The street I'm on is lined with shops and bars and restaurants. It's very clean. It's ten-thirty in the morning and the sidewalk is warm. I can bring Sara here. It fits the image I want her to have. The kids will have friends in big houses with gardens.

I check into an edge-of-town motel and make my first run through the bars. In the Glad Hand, a small one, I meet my first realtor. Hell, sure he can find me a place. He's playing a game with dice and cups. I watch him very closely.

By four o'clock the realtor and I are halfway up the hill behind Bridgeway. Bridgeway is the name of the main street. The house he's showing me is on a corner in trees. It overlooks the bay. The bay is a luminous painting. I'm so far from St. Louis I could be on another planet. I feel like I've finally jumped out of a net.

God, what a bridge. I cross it again going back to Malibu. I spend the night then move us out in the morning. Steve's in the back seat in our improvised nursery and Dave is in Sara's arms.

"Is it nice?"

"You have to see it. It isn't Salina, I'll tell you that."

"What's it like?"

"It's like the Mediterranean."

"Okay, Jack, what's that like?"

"Peaceful and beautiful on the water."

"Is there work around?"

"I've already got a job in the squid packing plant."

"You're kidding."

"Not at all. Squid packing is the local industry. It's great. The kids can start when they're five."

"Can't you just answer me?"

"Of course there's work. We're ten minutes from San Francisco. There's work everywhere."

"It's going to be all right, isn't it?"

"It's going to be great."

I feel like the placing of Sara and the kids in Sausalito is a step toward their protection. The place is right, now all I have to do is position myself near some money. The secret structures in my head are made of wire and light. Very solid, though. My commitment is very solid.

I'm still alone in there but that's okay. Being alone is my life. I'm the family's point-man. They aren't alone because I'm with them.

Sara isn't alone because she has me.

I really believe it.

When we're finished moving in I look around from our deck and realize what a good job I've done. "This is how it should be, Dad, this is how it's done."

I work in the city selling packaged tours. I get home late a lot. Sara holds dinner but lately she doesn't wait on the drinks. It's not like she's drunk when I come home, it's just she's been drinking. I'm a businessman coming home late.

She pours me a martini when I come in the door. I look forward to it. She pours herself one too, though, and lately, after three or four, she's been getting nasty. She's got it in her head that I'm unfaithful. I've been faithful since our marriage.

This time I'm driving home drunk and the traffic toward the bridge is thin and moving fast. When you're drunk the bridge is a fuzzed-orange comfort in the distance. I'm resentful. I don't need to put my time in the city and come home to abuse. My right hand is resting on Karin's head. Karin is my boss' Danish secretary.

I have to move my hand away when we hit the tollgate. I give the guy in the booth the money and a big smile. He turns away. He can see what Karin's doing with her mouth. I pull slowly out of the slot and put my hand on the flesh where Karin's hair ends. I stroke it gently. No big deal, tomorrow is Saturday, after all.

ELEVEN

Life isn't much anyway.

I mean you prepare for the real stuff, then you get it and all you have to do is keep it going the way it's supposed to. You have to worry about accidents but you can't do anything about them. You've got to be careful that what you're doing isn't dumb, but outside of that it's one foot in front of the other and after x number of years your life will be good. How you feel doesn't matter unless you let it get in your way. Sara lets it get in her way. Sara doesn't know how to drink. *And* she drinks too much. There's a place you've got to go in your head where the alcohol works *for* you. Hysteria is bullshit.

The ghost of my life the way it's supposed to be lays shiny tracks in my head. The alcohol regulates my speed. Surrounded by fake people in fake jobs, I'm a secret, solid Casey Jones. Maybe Sara isn't happy now. Maybe I do things I don't like myself for. Maybe I'm not always as nice a guy as I know I am. But right now the run is uphill. When we get to the top we'll coast. The strain is worth it.

I really don't have a lot in common with the people I deal

with to make money. Most of them drink. That's something. But there's still that feeling that if they found me out they'd be surprised. Maybe worse than surprised. I don't think any of them cry during *Pinocchio*. Maybe they do, I don't know. Sometimes somebody cries at the bar but it's usually not too hard to get him out of it. There's always some anger there too. The anger can save your ass when you get sloppy.

Our little girl is named Bridget. She's seven months old. Steve is four and Dave is two-and-a-half. I play with them every night when I'm home early enough. It's a beautiful house. But as a town to bring up kids in, Sausalito doesn't make it. The people are cold. Sara takes the kids to the little parks but none of the other women talk to her. She isn't stylish and the kids have haircuts she gave them herself. I'll get us out of Sausalito soon. Bridget is a beautiful little doll.

Drunk one night I'm watching Sara get ready for bed and I ask her why she never lets me see her breasts. "These are for the children," she says.

Our sex life is dull. It's uneventful. But if Sara's in an allright mood there's an hour or so of grace every night, right after dinner. In my chair with a drink and the mountain and bay outside in blue and purple darks, I'm pretty happy. When I get in my chair I take an inventory. I compare myself to other people. I'm doing pretty well and moving. The kids are asleep, so they're safe and comfortable.

Steve has bad dreams sometimes, but all kids have bad dreams. Sara, I guess, just isn't a very sexual woman. Karin goes too far, but that's what I need to keep my balance. She'll do anything. I'll do anything because I know I'm getting out of the job and probably won't see her again. I don't want to be unfaithful, but I'll do what I have to. My mind is supple. I can bend it around anything.

I remember the smell of the Chrysler in Harry Book's father's garage. I remember the black legs of my father's piano, and the sound coming down on me like a great, shuddering flower. When I'm like this I remember with my whole body and everything comes back. I remember how Caroline's hair smelled like the Castile shampoo in our bathroom. Conti Castile.

Karin at lunch time. I fucked her from twelve to one. She wore the same clothes back because she said she liked to be able to remember what we'd been doing. My boss is fucking her too. I have to be careful.

There are still some orchids in the old greenhouse that's off to the right of my house. My kids take their baths in a big, glossy, claw-foot tub.

The anger is there in the morning. I don't really think of it as anger. I think of it as the machine that keeps me moving. I've been throwing up every morning for a month. I have a towel on the front seat of my car in case I have to throw up on the way to the city. I go to the doctor about it but he wants to talk about my drinking. I'd rather not. I tell him I keep it under control by drying out every once in a while.

The last thing he says is that maybe I should sit down and figure out how much I drink a day when I'm drying out. He gives me a little sheet with alcohol equivalents on it. I do it for my own information. When I'm drying out I'm drinking about 22 ounces a day. When I'm not drying out I'm good for more than a quart.

I think I'll be a stockbroker. I can't handle the travel business any more. My boss caught me with Karin. He had to break down the door of her apartment to do it, but he caught us. I haven't been fired but things aren't the same. Stockbroking is a step up. It's better to say "I'm a stockbroker," than "I sell group tours." It's a higher class con.

I keep seeing women in the street and sometimes, when I'm hungover and horny in the morning, it's all I can do to keep from following. One I do follow. She comes to the office looking for a job and when she leaves I grab my coat and chase her out onto the street. She's really quite beautiful. I have to do it. She has an apartment on Greenwich, just off Union, and we bring up some groceries, wine and a bottle of bourbon. It's only eleven thirty in the morning. I lose it somewhere during the day, and I wake up naked in the moonlight. I'm stuffing a pair of menstrual-blood-stained shorts into my neighbor's hedge.

You have to have a sense of humor coming out of a black-out. The sense of humor is very important. The self-conscious, hangdog, Jesus-am-I-sick in the early-opening bar. There's a tacit sense of heroism in the air. We laugh at pain. We may fuck up but we pay our dues, don't we? The trick is getting out of the bar as soon as the edge is off. The day can turn ugly if you don't. I'm still a professional. I've got a family, and work to do.

I'm good at what I do. I've already made enough money to get the hell out of Sausalito. The new house is in Mill Valley. I buy it for $29,000. Mill Valley is a better place to live for the kids. The house is in a little canyon, steep and hidden in the redwoods. The kids call it "the spooky house."

I'm not a slob. I walk straight and my diction is good. I remember the shiny wetness of Dad's chin and the little steps he'd take to get across the floor. I walk straight no matter how drunk I am. I have it together and I don't even think about it. I worry, but I don't think. I don't need to be sober to sell. I don't know if I *could* sell sober. It's a good job, and I get sent to New York for three months of training.

Steve is in school now. He's a funny little kid. His eyes are bad and he has to wear pretty thick glasses. His vulnerability is my vulnerability. It's like Steve carries the whole defensive structure of my life out the door with him every morning. He *can* be hurt and I know it.

Dave is five and very sturdy. I don't feel I have to worry

about him as much. I'm immensely grateful for that. Bridget, as always, is my darling. She's only four but she lets me know how much she loves me, how much she loves it when I play with her. As far as discipline goes, I'm more than willing to let Sara be the ogre.

On Halloween Bridget gets dressed as a little old lady in a dressing gown. She has a cane and the makeup makes her look a bit Oriental. It's amazing how much like a little old lady she looks. She rests both hands on the top of her cane with her toes pointing out and heels close together.

I make up stories for my kids. The one that goes on the longest is about a guy named Johnny Shadow. They're all sad that I'm going away. There's no question about their loving me.

Sometimes I bring Sara flowers. I do before I leave for New York for the three months of training. In New York I'm perfectly contained.

When the 7th Ave. Local leaves Wall Street for the under-river run, the black man across from me takes off his jacket. There are blood stains on it. He wraps it into a ball and pushes it out the top of a window. He takes off his shoes and throws them out too, then sits back down. His eyes are yellow and bloodshot. He doesn't bother me. He's looking right at me and I feel like we know each other. He's not a threat. My suit and briefcase don't matter. We're talking to each other somewhere below that stuff. I get off at Clark Street and he's left by himself.

I meet Barbara Landau in Julius' in the Village.

The bartender tells me her name, then he smirks.

"They call her the Wolf Girl," he says.

I don't like him for it. I hope he can see it in my face.

Barbara is two seats down at the bar. She isn't striking or anything, but her face pleases me and she has a beautiful body, very slightly overweight. Her right hand is down the front of the pants of the guy next to her. I can just see her fingers moving in the cloth. I'm fascinated. Not by what she's doing but by how she is, and how she sits there with a cigarette tilted up in her left hand and watches the mirror. She's very much in her own world.

I catch her eyes in the mirror and say a mouthed, "Hi" with my reflection. She smiles at me and shrugs. Her right hand could be a friend's pet she's watching for the night. I point at her drink and she nods once, slowly, with a lovely smile. The guy next to her is talking to the guy next to him. I move over and sit on her left. I feel remarkably comfortable. She's Jewish, the daughter of a Connecticut doctor. The word for her body, she tells me, is zaftig. Her father threw her out and cut her off when she had an abortion. She's drunk, but it's only there in her eyes. They're bright and amused, and a little bit scared.

She takes back her right hand and lights another cigarette. The guy barely notices. I can remember how amused Mary's eyes used to get when she was pretending she didn't see my erection. She'd drag her fingers right to its outline then stop. Her eyes were always bright and amused. But they weren't soft and they didn't have an edge of fear in them. I've never known anyone as fast as I know Barbara. We leave together. She has the ability to hold on in the street without being awkward or brittle. I've never been so comfortable.

The old darkness of Brooklyn Heights.

She takes me all over the city. The most interesting bars. She knows the whole string section of the New York Philharmonic intimately. She's honest and clear and a pure joy to be with.

When I'm sick she shows up at my window at three in the morning. It's raining. Maternal sexuality comes off her in waves. She slips into bed with me and holds me through the fever.

I know I belong here and I know I won't get to stay. There is no way out of a Catholic marriage. There isn't even any way out of my accumulated images. Barbara loves me. She talks and she says what she means. Most of the time, anyway. She takes care of me and I seem to take care of her, though I'm not sure how that works.

In class we each have to make a final presentation. We have to break down a corporate structure in terms of chain of command, function, and effectiveness. Needless to say, I don't have anything prepared so I go to the board and draw out the chain of command for our South St. Louis treehouse. When I'm through the class is transported. My instructor is transported too. He sends a letter back to the coast saying that I made the most remarkable presentation he's ever heard and that I'm the finest natural salesman he's ever come across. I get taken to lunch by the head of the division.

My stock is very high and it's time to go home. All I can do is run. I don't tell Barbara anything, I just run.

On the plane back I drink in the bathroom. Airline drinks don't make it. I'm ashamed of myself. Another clot of anger sinks down into my belly. Fuck the church and fuck my marriage. It's a good thing I have my kids. The airport is a plastic dream. The moving walkways are threatening.

"God, you're a shit," Sara says. She's drunk. She has to learn how to drink or stop drinking.

"You like living like this Sara? You like the way things are? I don't have to put up with it. I work too hard. You could do it for the kids, at least you could do that."

"God, I hate you."

She has no fucking idea. She doesn't see what I see and she's so goddamn stubborn and vicious that no matter what I say I'm always wrong. At least now I know. It's not me at all. It's Sara.

When the kids have to hide and cry it breaks my heart.

She catches me up in this bullshit and I don't know what I'm doing, she just wears me down and before I know it things are broken and the kids are crying and all I can do is walk out. I don't believe this. Because I can't remember exactly what gets said, she takes advantage. She lays it all on *me* next day. Why don't I ever hear this outside? Nobody outside ever tells me I acted like a prick. No matter how drunk I get.

The kids cry a lot. Steve screams at us to stop. It's gotten to be a joke, my trips to the hardware store for wall-patch. I punch holes in the wall.

Our banister will never be right. I've pulled it out too many times. I haven't hit Sara, but we throw things at each other. I've tried to get into being a weekend handyman but it doesn't seem to be appreciated. The plate glass window in the kitchen gets broken twice in the same day. I begin to park in the trees by the kids' school at recess. I watch them to see if the other kids like them. Dave is fine but Steve wanders the schoolyard by himself. He never gets picked for anything. He has to stand on the side and watch. I don't know what to do. I sit at the end of the bar by myself.

Sara's a physically strong woman, when she hits me it hurts, so I hit her back and we scuffle around in the living room. She falls down. She just fell but she stays there because the kids are in the doorway and it looks bad for me.

God, what a bitch.

It's not like this every day. I mean, we can't be like this every day. We have a code. We pretend a lot.

My father dies in the late summer of the year. I go to St. Louis. The funeral parlor is in the neighborhood and I go straight there. I don't imagine Mom will be home. Pat's the first one to see me and she runs across the floor and throws her arms around my neck. It's the closest we've ever been.

Mom is in her own world. On the way to the hospital

she'd ridden with Dad in the ambulance. That's when he'd told her he'd always needed her. It was the best thing he could have said.

I stand in front of the coffin with nothing inside me. I'm conscious that he's better off dead. It isn't a feeling, but it's better than nothing. It's like looking at a statue fallen on the ground.

I call up Sara from St. Louis but I can barely hear her. There's loud music in the background and Sara's drunk. I'm angry at Sara.

At home again, the kids are in bed and I'm crying. It's taken me a month and a half. I've got a bottle of Tanqueray next to me and I can't stop. That I wanted to be proud of him and wanted him to be proud of me seem to come down to the same thing. I never got through. I never did.

I buy us a cottage on the lake at Tahoe. The kids love it.

I never really felt like I knew who I was, but now I don't even feel like the guy who didn't know. All the memories are there. They come up at the oddest, most painful times. More and more I know who I am because of the way my friends talk to me. That's okay too. I'm solidifying my place in the money-making structure. I'm becoming a fixture and that, I think, is the whole game.

It's unusual, but there is one night when I can't find my car. I can't really walk. That's even more unusual. I'm conscious that a car is following me. It's late, on the borders of Chinatown. A Chinese woman with heavy makeup is driving the car. She pulls up just in front of me and leans out of the window to ask if I have a problem. I tell her I've lost my car. She tells me to hop in and we'll look for it. She takes me to an alley off Grant. Right down to the end of the alley. There's a gold temple-top above us. She tells me she's a prostitute. I'm not interested. "I just want to find my car," I say. She gets out a gun from her purse and tells me to take my clothes off and get out. That's what I do. I can't say I'm frightened. I'm too far gone to be frightened. She takes my clothes and wallet and drives away. So I'm naked in a Chinatown alley. What the hell. I keep moving. At the end of the alley I find my clothes where she's thrown them.

It's pretty funny, really.

Two weeks later she calls me at Tahoe. She wants $200 or she'll tell Sara. Big deal. I already told Sara. I think it's funny as hell.

It's close to the wintertime. Every weekend we head up to Tahoe. We pick up the kids after school and drive straight through. We have set places we stop for food and drinks. We're not in terrific spirits when we get there. We seldom argue in the car on the way up. We just drive. But when we get to the lake we usually go out for a couple of drinks. By the time we go to bed things are tense.

Saturday the kids are outside and we work in the cabin. I'm *very* sorry for myself. Alone in the daylight hours, Sara and I have little or nothing to say to each other. At night it's different.

"I'm sick of you embarrassing me."

"Oh, fuck you, Sara. I'm a big boy. If you don't like my friends you can stay home."

"What makes you think your friends like you?"

"I don't give a fuck who likes me. Whatever I do it's better than sitting around here and letting you bore my ass off."

"You're such a shit. How could I marry you? You're such a goddamn shit."

"You did the best you could, okay? Now why don't you shut the fuck up and go to bed."

"You're such a shit."

I feel so sorry for myself that I catch myself whining in my head. I hate to do that. It's not how I want to be. Sometimes I think there's someone else in there who's trying to fuck me up.

In the morning there's not much time for anything but Church and the ride back. I'm so goddamn sick I feel like I've had cotter pins knocked out of my joints. They all hurt and they don't move right. The church is down the road a couple of miles. It's one of those new, half-hearted rustic jobs. It has a big parking lot. Churches don't look right with parking lots. I don't know how the kids feel about Church. I never asked them.

It's just a fact. Sunday we go to Church. I have a couple of drinks before I leave, but this one is bad. The church is big and woody. The priest is a visitor, a German Jesuit. I try to sit by the aisle but two kids wedge themselves in next to me. The priest has an axe to grind and I shudder inside. This is after the Ecumenical Council. The mass is in English now and he doesn't like it. Essentially, it seems, if we weren't all such depraved scumbags, this hideous violence would never have been done to the Mass.

He speaks good English. He's quite articulate. He's been running at the mouth for twenty-five minutes. And there I sit. From St. Mary Magdalen's to Lake Tahoe. There I sit and all I hear is the same old shit. I need a German to tell me about sin, right? I stand up in the pew. He pauses and looks at me.

"FUCK YOU!" I say, loudly.

I make my way out of the pew and up the aisle to the door. As I walk out I can hear that I'm getting a smattering of applause.

Early Erdmanns—Louis Karl, Arthur and Emil. Louis, George's grandfather, dead of DTs at 56. Arthur, George's father, who made his wine and beer in the basement. Emil, George's uncle, sold his father's Colt pistols for a pint of rye.

George and Marian, circa 1928. George is an alcoholic.

Jack, George, Pat and Marian, July 1, 1940. Jack is drinking Communion wine every Sunday. George is alcoholic, with an increasing dependence on prescription drugs.

Sara and Jack, New Year's Eve, New Orleans, '58. No comment.

TWELVE

This is 1970 and the gateway to the dark. I have one foot in and I'm poised, thoughtfully. The floor, of course, is moving. But I'm not aware of that. Sometimes I am, maybe, but I still associate a steady outside movement with luck and secrecy. To be quiet, skilled and secret in my head, and to move steadily on my own track. Without effort. To move steadily.

That's the worst thing about hangovers. You don't move steadily. You have to sit at the bar and be very still till the rush hits. Junkies talk about the rush. I get one too. When everything floats and you're sick like the world is made of invisible planes you have to slip through but can't, you're too clumsy, and you get down a double, maybe a second double, and all your centers glow at once and line up where they should be—that's a *rush*.

I'm not even afraid of the dark. I don't think there's much I'm afraid of. Except when I'm sick. I am afraid for Steve. Dave is my everyday hope. Bridget's my dream of apotheosis. Steve is my fear. I wonder how they talk together, when I'm not there. Christmas is upon me. The last week in November all of us shift into our Christmas modes. Some guys get sentimental but most get contained and resigned. And angry. The lights go up around Marin and the alcoholic families go into their slow, formal dance.

Ed, the afternoon bartender at Smiley's says, "Some drunks are like three-way bulbs, you know, they go up to 250 watts. Some are just steady 150's. The guys I always get are the flash-cubes. They go off once and that's it."

That's not me. I may modulate a bit, but I always throw out light.

Christmas comes down to the last minute, but I manage to get it all together. Christmas Eve we lay out a spread of cold cuts, salads, breads and liquors. We have the neighbors in, and when the last of them is gone I take a deep breath and get into the presents. It seems like all the kid's presents have to be assembled. Sara gets to bed before I do. We have lights around the windows and a big, full tree. I lie on the couch when I'm finished and look as deep into the lit-up tree as I can. I squint my eyes a bit to fuzz the lights. That's what I used to do at home.

The morning is great. I've done what I had to do and the kids are bouncing and jostling around the living room. The mood is wonderful, but by eleven o'clock it's beginning to get heavy. Sara's in the kitchen cooking. She's got a beer on the counter. I gave Steve a new fishing pole so I pack the kids in the car and take them over to Elephant Rock in Tiburon. It's a place where kids fish. I've got a fifth of cognac in my deep raincoat pocket. I lean above the water and drink. It gets late and grey and cold, but I can't leave. My eyes are locked in a seam between the grey sky and the grey water. I just can't leave.

Steve calls Sara and pretty soon my friend George comes down to pick us up. He leads me away. I need some sleep.

We leave my car where it is. On the way back the kids have nothing to say.

Dinner is ready at home but all I can do is go to bed. I hope I sleep till the morning. I don't want to wake up in the night. You can't *do* anything in the middle of the night. It feels like everything has gone wrong and now you're awake by yourself with nothing you can *do* about it. Sara is very gracious with George. Sara is always gracious with our friends. Steve comes in and asks me if I'm all right. Sure, I'm all right. I was just up too late. He stands there.

"Thanks for the pole, Dad."

"Yeah. You better get your dinner before it gets cold. Maybe we'll do something tomorrow. Think about what you'd like to do, okay?"

"Sure, Dad."

That night Sara's snoring. I suddenly have remarkable strength, and I flip the mattress onto the floor with her under it. She drags herself out with a bloody nose. She doesn't say a word, she just looks at me. I can't see her eyes but I can see the blood on her white nightgown. I put on a coat and go out on the deck. The canyons are very old. Redwood forests are very black at night. I need to get away for a while. The air in Tahoe isn't as thick.

It's not like I ever claimed not to be crazy. Sara knew a lot about me when we got married. She knew enough. It's not like anyone was misled.

I hate twilight. Twilight's the time I most like to spend in the bar. I feel like I'm ready to panic at twilight. It's alright to leave the bar and go out into the night, but it's not all right to go out into the half-night. In the bar I'm well-liked. But twilight. I don't know what the hell that is. It just scares me.

It isn't anybody's fault. I know that. Sometimes I know that. I'd tell Sara that if I were ever around her in just the right mood. It doesn't happen. She's so goddamn vicious she starts baiting me as soon as I walk in the door. There was something *strange* about her family. If I let her, she'd kill me. I think one of the problems is that I've become a mature drinker and she hasn't.

I mean, it's a matter of maintenance. I get a lot from alcohol but I sure as hell don't expect to get the kind of highs I got when I was a kid. They just don't happen. If Sara could get to where I am, things might be a lot better. I don't drink so I can spill my guts, I drink because I like it, and because it makes the day go faster. When I stay with my alcohol, calmly, it moves me through my life with a minimum of effort. Look at this house. How does she think we got it? How does she think we got the two additions and the cabin in Tahoe? If she'd just do that. If she'd just admit that I know what I'm doing.

Maybe I should take her away somewhere. Just for a while. Probably it's better to get away by myself first, get my head clear. This shit is choking me. I wish we could just love each other. It doesn't seem like all that much to ask. I wish we had that kind of dignity, you know, Donna Reed and Jimmy Stewart. Fuck it. I just need some space. Just for a while.

I'm working for Walston and Co. I convince them that what I should be doing is running a branch office in Incline Village at Tahoe. It is what I should be doing. Sara and the kids can keep coming up on the weekends and I can work on the house and get that extra room built. I need to get away.

When Sara comes up on the weekends, things aren't too bad. We're only a hundred yards from the lake. If I want to I can walk down there in the morning and look at it. "Goddamn, what a lake." What can you say? I find myself making simple pronouncements in my head. "Right, Jack, right. That's the way to get it done."

The Chamber's Lodge bar is a few blocks east. It's right on the lake. Good bar. Manager is a great guy. Off-season drinkers are always a cut above vacationers. From the deck the Sierras are so solid and cold it's like they skin your eyes. It's the kind of landscape lets you feel that just looking at it is doing something. In a vague way it makes me feel that anything I do in an orderly fashion is heroic.

I have a lady friend in Tahoe. Everything is great.

Sara doesn't have any idea. She brings the kids up on weekends and we get along. My mind and life are moving away from her like one of the boats on the lake. But Sara is sly. It's something I can't afford to forget. There isn't any chance I'll forget it. Sara sells the house in Mill Valley and comes to stay.

It always was the plan, I guess. I just chose to put it out of my mind. Within a week the tension in the house is a soundless, jamming static. Unless we're fighting, the kids keep pretty much to themselves. When we're fighting they hide, or cry, or scream. A guy at the bar tells me he caught Steve and his son smoking dope by the campground. I'll have to talk to Steve about it. The time just isn't right.

Between the traveling and the strain, I'm up to two fifths a day.

My chest is ringed like a dart board in bright, livid colors. By the water at Chamber's Lodge one night, I fell on an underwater piling. Perfectly flat on the round of the piling, right on my chest. Drunk. The colors are truly brilliant.

I'm beginning to get the feeling that the kids are happier when I'm not around.

Even Bridget.

Sometimes she looks at me like she's trying to pretend I'm not really there. She's only eight.

I figure about a third of every day is a blackout. You really need to trust yourself to face that. You need to know you're together. My lady friend wants to marry me. In the fluorescent bathroom light in her Incline Village apartment, I can't imagine why. The mirror this morning is as clear as I ever want to see it. This Is My Face, and Where Did I Go? My face is a weight. I carry it around.

My clothes are gone from the side of the bed. The window to the deck is open. It's freezing. She's thrown my clothes off the deck and into a snow bank. Spring and summer weren't much. Jesus. There is no point in feeling sorry for yourself. I sit down and pour a drink. I better get this together.

Christmas is coming again.

I've closed a deal, my only one, and made $8,000. I've begun to worry about keeping money in my pocket. I need to protect my supply. Occasionally I buy the kids presents. That costs money too. And eating. I have to eat. The hard thing now is knowing when I'm going to be drunk. Sometimes I'll drink for days and be fine. Sometimes two drinks in the morning wipe me out.

I still talk carefully. I still walk straight. I just have to be careful about tripping. It must be something to do with peripheral vision.

I'm still glib enough, in fact, to seduce my own wife. With wine, music and flowers. It's old business. I treat her like a whore in bed and she seems to love it. "Well," she says, "what have *I* been missing all these years."

She did love it and my stance is a little shaky. I seem to have won but I haven't. The Maison de Ville rises up in my head like a stone road-marker.

I'm gone from Walston & Co. With my $8,000. I'm not worried about work. I'm a great salesman. I only have to be sure that I don't let the money run too low.

It's almost Christmas now, and I'm driving back to Sara and the kids. This is the worst hangover I've ever had. The way I drink it can only mean that this time I nearly killed myself. But my friend Max has pills. He has a whole medicine chest full of pills. He gives me a handful of something. I take two right away. They seem to work. I don't really approve of people who take pills. I keep remembering that I have to talk to Steve. I remember my father's pill bottles. Fat and soft and crying in the middle of all his bottles. When a pain comes now it hits like an ax blow and fades fast. George Sanders in *Ivanhoe* with a mace. My armor cracks and I vibrate.

I need the pills because Sara and I are going to a Christmas party. Why are we going to a Christmas party? I have no fucking idea and neither does she. We still pretend. When we don't want to think, or live in the world, we pretend. Sara has other motives too. We haven't had a real good fight in quite a while.

I'm drinking as much as I can but nothing seems to be happening. Just past the periphery of the pills, I still feel like death. Sara is having a great time. Sara loves to flirt. Especially in front of me. Every goddamn party we go to she makes this imbecilic, high-school-girl attempt at charming every man in the room. I'm supposed to stand in the corner and feel terrible because Sara is sitting on Hal Glover's lap and whispering in his ear. Fucking cunt. Fucking viscious, self-centered, pea-brained cunt. I look out the kitchen window for a while. There's a light snow falling and there are Christmas lights receding through the dark trees. The gin I just tried has a nice, clean taste. Tanqueray always was a clean gin. I'll switch to gin for the night.

Sara's got one hand on Jerry Brandt's waist. She sways to the music like they were dancing. He's not moving. She whispers something to him on tiptoe. She loves to whisper in front of me.

I go to the bedroom and get our coats.

I stop in the kitchen for a quick one.

With Max's pills, it seems like I could drink forever and never show it.

I ease in behind Sara and cup her elbow with my hand.

"We better get going."

"You can go if you want."

"I don't feel too well, Sara. I don't want to drive in the snow feeling sick."

"Why don't you go lie down?"

"Look, if you want to come back you can. But I need a ride home, okay."

"Oh, shit," she says to Jerry.

Saying goodbyes at the door she's bright and pleasant.

She slams the door on the car.

"That's the last time you do this to me, you shit."

"What's your fucking problem, Sara?"

"You can't stand it. You know I'm having a good time and you're such a prick, it drives you crazy."

We're rolling down the driveway.

"Put your goddamn headlights on."

"But Sara isn't allowed to have a good time. Sara better fucking get taken home in case she has a good time."

Her voice has metal in it.

"Fuck off, Sara. Just drive me home and do what you want."

"That's a laugh. Do what *I* want. We never do what I want. In 13 years we never did what I want."

"What is it this time? Is it Jerry Brandt? You wanna go back and fuck Jerry Brandt? Go. Let me out here."

"Why wouldn't I? Why shouldn't I fuck somebody? Even when you can get it up I don't want to fuck you, you limp-dick fucking professional-failure. Not anymore. You don't tell me anymore. You're a goddamn failure with a soft dick and you can go fuck yourself with it."

We're weaving in the snow.

"You're a sad, dumb cunt, Sara, and I think you better go back to the party and find out that if you're really lucky some guy might let you fuck him behind the kitchen door. That's it, Sara. Behind-the-kitchen-door-job-party-cunt."

She gets calm.

"We hate you, don't you know that? We all hate you. You know what Bridget said to me? She said I wish Daddy didn't smell so bad sometimes. You want to buy her some more fucking presents maybe you should get her a nose-plug."

She laughs.

"Why don't you just fucking die," she says, "why don't you just fucking do it?"

I hit her on a full swing with the back of my hand on her mouth.

"You rancid fucking cunt. You flabby-ass rancid cunt."

She hits me in the mouth with the heel of one of her shoes. We're off the road and she's flailing at me.

"I hate you. Fuck. I hate you."

We run over something and she stops. There's a gap.

"Fuck."

I get out and walk around to the front of the car. I kneel down in front and bend my head to see what we hit. It's just a rise of snow. Sara hits the accelerator and knocks me back and to the side. I'm on my back and I can hear her moving the car. She's backing up for another shot. I scramble for the snow berm the plows have pushed up at the side of the road. The headlights swing around to me and I jump and flatten on the side of the bank just as the car hits six inches below my feet. I'm slipping and Sara is backing up again. We're both screaming and lights are going on in houses. She guns it again but I'm off to the side and running. There's a house across the street and I'm running so heavy and hard the sky and the trees and the house lights are snapping and pounding.

Sara's still screaming and I can hear a siren to my left.

The man on his porch is stringing Christmas lights over his door. He turns half-way as I tumble up the steps. The door is open and I lunge into his living room. I'm half-down on his rug. The siren is getting closer. I scramble on all fours to the back of his armchair. When I peek out he's standing there on the porch with a string of light dangling in the snow.

"Hide me," I say.

THIRTEEN

"Forget it, Jack. You're not coming in."

"This is my goddamn house and nobody keeps me out." She's calm again.

"Go away."

I can be calm too. I walk around the side of the house to the woodpile and come back with a good-sized log. I throw it through the glass door. Steve has come to the upstairs balcony and he's screaming, "God, please stop it, please." Clearly, I need my own place.

I start the next day at the bar. I sit quietly and listen to the stories. Somebody's wife tried to run him down. It's pretty goddamn funny. You just need the right perspective.

I'm still a little scared. The thing to do is act on the moment. This is the day to get out. I imagine my gesture as large and somehow grand. I talk to the kids one at a time. I drive to the shore with each, one at a time, and explain as best I can.

Dave's eyes fill with tears. I tell him I'll be living in Carnelian Bay. It's only eight miles away, but it's too far for him.

Steve is relieved. He can't take any pleasure in it because that's not allowed. But I'm sure he's relieved. He must be.

Bridget says "Oh."

The way the kids look. The way their faces get farther away. I look at Bridget and I see the idea of Bridget. I can't stop what happens. I can't even slow it down. I remember the afternoon in Mill Valley when Sara fell. The kids came up the staircase to the door and Steve was in front. The oldest in front. His face was trying so hard to show me how it felt. How all of it felt. The others stood behind him. I've asked too much of Steve. I wanted him to be happy. I can still make him happy. From outside I can do more. If I'm outside Sara won't be able to push my buttons quite so easily. Anything can happen, everything is possible. Unusually, that seems positive this morning. It's funny how a decision can change your mood.

Doesn't matter what it is.

It's a very grey day and I feel like my life has been simplified. I mean, this is a joke and the only answer is divorce.

The Mouth Martini isn't really my own invention, but it might as well be. I don't know anyone else who drives this way. I have my vodka and vermouth and I mix them in my mouth while I'm driving. W.C. Fields used to do that.

I get a Carnelian Bay apartment. I take a wonderful shower. I think of myself as a stylish, monied bachelor. I'll have a liquor cabinet and food in the refrigerator. My clothes will stay in my closet. I'll need to find a job but not right now. If I play this right I can take care of everything for the next six months. Get the machinery going. The steam in the shower is marvelous. I slip out naked and run to the kitchen. I have a pint of Hennesey's and six glasses. I pour myself a healthy drink and take it back to the shower. Cognac in the misted, hot air. The lake out the window.

The divorce is final June 21st, 1972. Things get vague. I

come out of a blackout across the room from a naked woman who's playing the accordion. She's a prostitute. She tells me I'm the only trick she's ever had who really wanted to hear her play.

There's always another place to be. I think of myself as between engagements. A holiday of sorts. Something is going to happen, and when it does I'll be ready. The Waiting Game has never failed me before. I'm caught up in a minor whirlwind. When it blows itself out I'll pick up the pace of real-life again.

What I really need, I think, is some time to heal. I feel more than a little damaged.

Gene lives in Shingle Springs with his wife. I'm always welcome. Alcoholic husbands and wives like company. And I'm a great guy. The guy with the tattoos told me. His eyes filled with tears across the booth from me and he said, "Jack, you're an incredible human being." He gave me two hundred dollars to gamble with. This was in Reno. Even his bald head had tattoos on it. Gene is a lot sicker than I am.

Gene's put me in touch with some guys who'll be building a development around Shingle Springs. Easy money. Sales skills.

I'm driving to Reno one night when I hear the symphony for the first time. Magnificent, with swelling strings and reeds. It's all so crafted, so melodic. It fills the car as if my head is growing. It's my secret life made real. I know now the depth of beauty in my head. I've got myself a gallon cooler. I fill it with ice, beer, and those canned, pre-mixed screwdrivers.

I'm not really sure how I get into the mental hospital lock-up in Auburn. I guess I pushed it too far. Live and learn.

They let me out three days later but not before the doctor told me I came in with a blood-alcohol content of .45. Dead, really.

The houses are actually getting built in Shingle Springs,

and I have enough money to protect my supply. Mac the Welder is my favorite guy in town. I like to sit and drink with him in his long, low, falling-down ranch house. His yard is a mass of engines, axles and rusted wheels. The chickens seem happy. Mac bitches about his sister. His sister came by and threw out the little green guys. They were the nicest little guys you'd ever want to meet, he says. They drank with him and told great stories. They were too small for the chairs so they'd sit in funny places. The bitch scared them off. They'll probably never come back. There are tears in his eyes.

I walk in on Gene in the middle of a seizure. He's foaming and purple with a gash on his head. I can't get help with the phone. The hospital says, "Wolfman again, huh? Tell him to call his doctor. We're not picking him up." His doctor says, "Fuck him. He's costing me a fortune." I get some liquor down him and he comes out of it. We send him to a recovery house in Camino.

While he's away I pick up my kids and bring them down to Shingle Springs for a barbecue with Gene's kids. The bonfire gets built too close to the picnic table so that when I fall backwards off the bench, I land in the fire and burn off the back of my parka. Steve goes to sit in the car.

At a fund-raising fair outside Reno two nurses will take your blood pressure for free. They make me sit down and run to get a doctor. The doctor checks me straight into the Veteran's Hospital for two weeks. Getting a drink in the Veteran's Hospital is complicated. I have to steal my clothes, sneak through the hospital halls and out a window to my car, and drive three blocks to a liquor store. I get back, and back in my gown, and back in bed.

In Tahoe Sara won't let me in.

"Okay, Sara. I'll go to the campground. Tell the kids in the morning."

"Go to hell."

The campground won't be bad. The cop didn't get the bottle in my sleeping bag. I travel with a one-man tent. It's in the back with my vodka. I feel resigned, like I said, and I actually take the trouble to set it up. Sugar Pine Campground, covered in snow.

Steve comes by in the morning. He's fourteen, and his eyes have a fixed, pained skepticism in them. His glasses, I think, make him look older. Maybe not.

"Hey, Dad."

"Steve. How's it goin' buddy?"

"It's okay. I can't stay."

"I know. I should have called and said I was coming. I never do, do I?"

"No, not really."

He's not moving, just looking at me.

"Is there anything I can do for you, Dad?"

"Not really, I was just heading up to Reno and it got too thick to drive."

"You want to come back to the house?"

"I don't think your mother wants to see me. Next time I'll call ahead."

He watches me very closely, as if he's trying to remember something.

"Yeah. I gotta go."

"See ya, kid."

"Yeah."

I order another double vodka over in Reno and the bartender looks at me blank.

"No way."

"What's that mean?"

"It means no way. Go sleep it off."

Told to go home in a Second St. lounge. I look at myself in the mirror before I leave.

The motel ceiling has those rotten little sequiny flecks in

it. A mottled stucco surface with little colored flecks. It takes me a while to figure it out. This is my room. It's okay. I paid for this room and it's mine. The chintzy night-table has an unopened pint of Smirnoff in it. I'm breathing easier. I knock off a few ounces and jump, violently, as a shadow moves across the drapes. I get in the shower with my bottle. I didn't even get to see my kids.

I get out of the shower without having washed. I don't remember till I sit down on the edge of the bed. I can't go back in there. I wash my armpits over the sink, and sit back down on the bed.

I put down my bottle and hit myself across the face, hard, with my open right hand. I'm watching myself in the mirror. I don't flinch. If I get my hand up and back as far as my shoulder, I can hit my cheek pretty hard. I hit it until it's a bright red. The other half of my face is red too, but not the same. It cracks pretty loud in the bare room.

FOURTEEN

My car is my life and my hope. It gets me where I want to go.

Sometimes I'm wrong though. Like now I'm in Reno. Fuck Reno. Fuck Sara.

Reno threw me in jail and stole my clothes. It wasn't Reno stole my clothes, not really, it was yesterday's hitchhiker. I picked him up outside Vallejo on the freeway ramp with this white cardboard sign that said, "We Are All God's Children."

He got my watch too.

Across the street from the grey and white Reno police station is a white iron railing. It fronts on the Truckee River. I lean on the rail for a moment to get my bearings. If I go up to Second and turn right, Second takes me to Keystone. My car is probably on Keystone. The sun is still out and it's all my head would hold. The way I'm feeling I have to hold onto simple images. Images of places are easy. One place drains down to reality and the next fills my head with promises of safety and well-being. I'll get to my car and get back to San Francisco, and by tonight I'll be in a small, controlled space with a bottle and maybe a woman to put her hands on me. I'll really be able to sleep.

It's going to be a long walk in the heat so I pick up a pint of vodka at an off-sale bar on Second. On Second, Reno is all around you like a clownish, baggy misery. The colors are clown colors and the mountains at the end of the street are drawings of mountains. Just off the curb at the corner, a very fat blonde woman in a Giants' cap and tight T-shirt is standing on tiptoes yelling "Howie!," her hands cupped at her mouth. Her T-shirt, unbearably, says "Don't Play With The Knobs." She's clear and bright in the sun. I turn in toward a storefront and have my first drink. It's a long walk. The curbs throw me occasionally but I am, after all, free and holding a bottle. And I'm well-dressed. If I keep it together I have it made.

The car is on Keystone about six blocks from the Keystone Lounge. The clothes are still gone but at least I'd hidden my money. I drive a slow six blocks and turn off the car. I still have the ragged-ghost feeling. It feels like you're not quite there, that your flesh is too light and doesn't fill the right holes. There was a time when the first shot would hit and pull together a tight center in my belly. It's not like that anymore.

I put my bottle under the seat and both of my hands on the steering wheel. I rest my head on the chrome of the horn. My hands hurt. When the guy in the drunk tank had stopped pounding the padding on the walls and turned around to me, I could see he was really crazy. When he started toward me with his right fist pointing, I got up and went to the wall on my side, and began to pound the padding. He joined me and we pounded it together. I lost some skin from my knuckles.

Later, when he gave it up and went back to lying face down on the floor, the bald guy with the tapering head put his hand on my shoulder, turned me over, and gave me a serious wet kiss. I hit him on the mouth and he fell back on his haunches with a hurt, betrayed look.

I hated punching him. It made me twist in my head.

I get out of the car and into the rotten Nevada heat. I walk as if I were following a set of those dance-instruction, cut-out feet. The Keystone's made of cinder blocks and they come out of some wrecked shrubbery. They're enameled a bright red. It's dark inside, so I stand in the doorway till I can see. On the short side of the bar, closest to the door, are swivel chairs instead of stools. An old woman sits in one of them. She hasn't put her teeth in, and her profile sinks into her mouth. The bartender's face comes swimming up and looks at me. He looks at me as if I were someone else. It feels to me like he's looking at someone else. I asked for a double, my vodka, before I got to the bar. He brings it to me without saying anything, and puts it in front of me with the reluctance bartenders can let you feel with just a slight hitch in the serving arm.

"They threw me in the tank," I say.

"You earned it."

He goes back to the sink at the dark end.

When I call him back for another, he tells me I'm going to die. That it takes the system a certain time to detoxify, and that if you start again before it's had the chance, the alcohol content in your blood goes way up. Beyond a certain point your system just kicks out and you die.

I like him. He's an older, sweet-tempered German. I feel deeply sentimental that he's worried about me so I tell him not to, that I really don't have much of a problem. I tell him I'm just a periodic drunk, every six months or so. It feels like I'm a nice guy, and doing him a favor, shielding his feelings with a certain delicacy. All I have to do is get back to the city and dry out, I tell him. I even drink some coffee. I go into the bathroom and look at my face in the mirror. I wash my armpits with the smelly pink soap from the dispenser. I get dressed again and laugh a little. "Look good, smell great." I go out to the bar and turn on the con in earnest. When I finally hit the street, it's dark. I have a quart of vodka with me, off-sale.

At the back of my head the voice is telling me simple, paralyzing things. "You'll kill yourself or you'll kill somebody else. You'll spend the rest of your life in jail." At the front of my head, where the images are, it's all "Safe now. Feel that weight in the bag, you're safe."

Highway Eighty, going south, has a wide sweep to it. The dark only breaks once in a while. I don't get all that far. The vodka gets me as far as Verdi. I have the side vent open and I can hear things on the air. Roaring voices are stretching vowels in a static underlay. I pull off and into Verdi. There's not much there. I'd try a parking lot but my head is full of cops' flashlights, and I know I'll never be able to sleep in my car.

I cross under the freeway to the river. I know a spot with a little grove right down from the road. I'll hear the water rushing and be able to go to sleep. It's beautiful out, and moonlit, and I drop my sleeping bag in the grove. I have plenty of liquor and the night is starry and deep. All I have to do is lie down.

I smooth out my vinyl-covered sleeping bag and snuggle in. I start to drink in the direction of passing out. When I finally do, the sleep is white. A white sleep is when you seem to be asleep but your head is noisy, and crowded. There's a shifty, flat-white light in it, like the moon is inside your eyelids.

Everything inside is constricted. Jail, and Reno, and the sides of the sleeping bag. I must have rolled and thrashed because toward sunrise my sleeping bag, turned now with its foot toward the river, slides gently on pine needles down and into the Truckee River. The icy water rushes into the bag and I'm awake again with my nerves screaming. Jesus, it's cold. I push and kick my way out of the bag and stand there in the cold ropes of the water. I start my push to the shore and half-way there the fear hits. Maybe I knocked the bottle over. Self-pity wells in my eyes. "Please God, just this once, God, please! Don't let the bottle be empty!"

It's the halflight part of the morning, in rivermist, but some things are very clear. There are bits of shiny mulch on my hands. My eyes are tender and sharp, and right at the bank with one knee in the mud and the other foot trailing in the water, I look up the slope at the bottle. It's just standing there, oversized in the mist. I stay the way I am, in gratitude. When I finally slog up the bank, I pull the bottle to my chest and slump against a tree.

I sit cross-legged. As I dry out and drink and get warm, the sun comes up and makes me feel perfectly, ridiculously, safe.

The thing about coming out of a blackout is that when you come out in a strange place there's a period of time that goes by before you know anything. Your heart gets slow and your eyes watch. It used to be popular to talk about "existential dread." Well, coming out of a blackout is *it*. You don't remember anything, that's a given. You don't know where you are, or why you're surrounded by strangers. Sometimes it's a while before you know who you are.

You feel like you have to make yourself up. You're in the middle of a sentence, talking to a pile of coats. You're bending over, and lacing up strange shoes.

This one, though, isn't too difficult. Not like the last one when I came out of it behind the wheel of a moving car. I'm in a padded cell and that, at least, makes some sense. I'm alone. It's not a drunk tank. The metal door has a small window in it, wavy glass and rippled wire strands. I'm not restrained, I'm just in a cell. When a blurred head goes by the window, I go to the door to see.

Most of the outside is a dull, grey-green. That's the other wall of the corridor. Set in it and moving away to the right are three other doors, one red, one blue and one green. There are faint voices down there.

I've got a bed and the room is very high. The one window is high too. I'm still drunk, I think, or maybe I'm crazy. It's better to be crazy than drunk. People think better of you. I can't have been here too long. I lie down. On my back I can see the top of a pine tree through the high window. I think like cotton. Like the cotton in my head or the mouth of an aspirin bottle. I'll just lie here. I don't have to do anything yet. I don't have to make myself up yet. It's out of my hands. This isn't a jail, it's a hospital. They have drugs and when I come down it won't be bad on clean sheets.

Sara's in Tahoe. She won't come. There was a time it was always easy to make her laugh, but not any more. Now it's throwing things or trying to kill me. Sara's in Tahoe. Woodsy in the house with the piney sliding glass she broke. She'll stay there and drink her goddamn beer. The hell with me. She'll tell the kids what a sorry son-of-a-bitch I am, but they'll know better. I am sorry for myself. I have every goddamn reason. But this might be all right. This is a real crisis and proves there's something wrong. If Sara can see that, then maybe when I play it right, I'll put it back together. I have to see my kids. They know I've always tried. The time in the blizzard it took a lot. Sara'll know that it's all real now. That I'm almost dead but still trying. She has to know I'm still trying. That must count for something. Maybe she cries. I hope so. I'm in the hospital so there's a chance I nearly died. If I had just a couple of drinks I could think better. At least I'm not like Dad and given up. The thinking will always come back. I'll never get that goddamn fat. Fat and soft in his hospital room. I'm not like that and I want my kids back. The way it used to be. They were small and helpless and they liked me the way I played with them and brought them stuff. If I play this right I can work it. I'll just have to tell Jeannie and she'll have to understand. About the kids. She doesn't have kids but she's got her animals. I'm not a lousy father, whatever else I am. I swore I'd never be like that. Maybe the hospital called Sara and she'll drive down. Pretty soon they'll tell me how I got here. I'm not in jail so I didn't wreck the car. I remember I was wet and talking on the phone. I remember that. The phone booth was lit up and green. I was in the river and then I was talking on the phone. Verdi, no, I must have driven back. I didn't do anything serious because I'm not in jail. It's better to be crazy anyway. I'll lie here and close my eyes. Verdi the composer. The car radio. Fuck it.

Precipitating Stress:

This 44 year-old, white male was admitted on Monday, 9/13/76. He was transported by the Reno Police Department. He said "I want to die," and laughed.

The patient is a heavy user of alcohol, drinking heavily from age fifteen onward, that is, twenty-nine years. For the past month, the patient has been drinking one quart or more of vodka a day. He reports that he has no trouble sleeping.

I wake up when the door opens. The orderlies come in, white and trim with black, army-surplus-store shoes. They're both in their twenties, and stocky. One stays by the door, casual, and the other comes over, looks down at me, and puts his hands in his white-coat pockets.

"How do you feel?"

"Not too bad. How long have I been here?"

"They brought you in last night."

"The police?"

"That's right."

"Where's my car?"

"It's in the pound. You didn't need a car."

"What hospital is this?"

"Nevada State Mental Institution, Ward 6."

I'm rubbing my forehead heavily with the back of my left hand. The words are coming easily. I never make trouble. I'm always low-key with the authorities.

"I guess I was pretty bad. I don't remember."

No shock treatments. That's what Dad let them do.

"I wasn't here but I read the log. Says you were good for six months' intensive. You don't look that bad to me."

"Does anybody know I'm here?"

"I don't know. The police had a lot of complaints. Your mother probably knows."

This one turns my stomach.

"My mother's in St. Louis."

"Yeah. But you called her up to let her know you were going to kill yourself. She called the police, too."

"What others?"

"A few casino guards. A Denny's manager. For Reno, you made an impression."

The guy by the door just leans there.

"They got you in a phone booth on South Wells. Right across from Denny's. You were sitting in the bottom of the telephone booth, crying, with a couple of bottles and a carving knife."

I don't say anything.

"Your blood alcohol was .36. They had to shoot you up with valium to get you quiet."

"What happens now?"

"That's up to you. Can you walk?"

"I think so."

"We'll take you out on the ward."

"How big is it?"

"You and eight others."

I'm off-balance when I get up. I already feel that I've moved into my part. The orderlies arrange themselves on either side and help me into the hall. The doors on the other side are bright colors. The ceiling is even higher than mine and the hallway is long, from door-to-door maybe eighty feet. Right in its middle the walls break out and open into a large, airy hexagon. Against one wall in the open area is a raised platform surrounded by heavy, reinforced glass. There's a nurse at a desk inside. A black man in pants and pajama top is watching me from a chair by the television. Someone's coming up behind me. He glides by in pajamas. He comes to the first face of the hexagon, turns, follows it to the next, turns, follows it behind the television, turns at the next and crosses the hallway to the other side. His eyes are level and bright. He has the intensity of a figure skater.

"Well, Mr. Erdmann. I think I'll call you Jack, if that's all right."

"Certainly."

"Now the doctor will see you in an hour or so and I'd like you to just relax and feel free to read or watch television or just sit."

She's a pleasant enough woman. One side of her caramel hair is ruffled out as if she's had some trouble.

"Can I use a phone?"

"Oh, I don't think so, Jack. Not yet."

The black man is still looking at me.

"Don't let Henry bother you. He'll say something when he's ready."

I take the cracked, fake leather armchair by the window. One orderly stays and talks to the nurse, and the other leans on the wall two windows away. It's a bright day and I can see the mountains and the red-brick side of the next building.

My mother called the police. I drove back to Reno from Verdi with my liquor. That was sunrise and they brought me here at night. Maybe my head just knew I needed to dry out, and set this whole thing up so I could do it in a hospital. That happens. My clothes are the same, not really dirty, just crushed. It's strange that everything in the room seems drained of color to an exact degree of flatness. When I think of the outside it's thick and deep. In here it's just flat.

Henry is looking at me and I realize in a very long instant that in order to look at the front of my pants I've fanned them out with two fingers on each hand, pulling each seam at the thigh. I'm caught in the start of a little girl curtsey, and I shrug reflexively.

Henry nods.

The walker is passing behind me again. It's his third circuit.

Henry is still nodding. There's just an edge of recognition in his eyes. Like he knows me or something. I feel slightly panicked.

From the hallway I haven't been down yet, a woman in a pink cotton dress, brown socks and brown loafers scuffles into the room. Her legs are swollen and she doesn't have any teeth. Her hair is done in Shirley Temple ringlets. Oklahoma, I think.

I'm the only one in street clothes. She comes straight to me.

"Doctor?"

Her voice is southwest. I feel right, and proud.

"Doctor, could you wrap my legs up, please? I think it's time they got wrapped."

"I'm not a doctor."

"Oh."

"I'm sorry."

"You can't wrap my legs?"

"No."

"Oh. Well then."

She turns and looks around but there's only Henry, the walker, and the nurse in the cage.

Henry says, "Her legs hurt her bad."

"I can see."

"My mama used to get to where her legs hurt like that."

"It must be bad."

"Yeah, things get fucked up."

"Yeah."

"It got like I wanted to hurt my family."

"You don't want to do that."

"Yeah. But that's the way it got. That ain't me. I told them, even, so they got me here and that's okay, where I should be. It's like I got a flu, like a fever. I got to where I told Joyce and she went up and took my gun. I mean that's not me. The kids crying in the kitchen. I'm not like that, you know."

"Yeah, I know."

I do know.

"Well, you be cool too, then."

I know the nurse is watching us and I can feel my inspired amateur stance coming on.

Quietly, the woman with the legs is back.

"Doctor?"

"I'm not a doctor."

I say it like I just never bothered to get licensed.

"Doctor. I can't masturbate anymore. You know it just doesn't work anymore."

My voice is very calm and I tell her, "Well, why don't you go back and try again. And let me know what happens."

Henry smiles a little. He has big hands he keeps on his knees. The walker glares as the woman cuts across his path.

He has an almost perfectly round, monkish bald spot. The quiet orderly comes by with some tea. Very sweet, with honey. It's a good prop, and I needed a prop. With my tea I look serene. Henry's not talking.

In ten minutes the woman is back.

"I want to thank you doctor, so much. It worked this time. Just like that."

"I'm really not a doctor you know. I'm a priest."

"I'm still a Catholic, Father."

"Bless you then."

"Would you bless me, Father?"

"I just did."

"I didn't hear you, Father, but thank you."

"Bless you my child."

"Well now. Thank you so much."

Mental Status:

No evidence of delusion or hallucinations. He is incoherent at times, but this can be attributed to his recent use of alcohol. He has serious grandiose tendencies, and tends to drop names—like the President's, and Governor of California.

The day fades out like that, fuzzy and strange with non sequiturs hung in the air like mines. I don't care. I've got it figured. This is where I dry out again. When they shoot me up with valium again, I know I'm in the right place. Every once in a while a hole opens up in my head. I close it up again.

Next morning the nurse tells me I'm incredible, I came out of it so fast. The way I was when I came in, it's hard to believe.

Before lunch I get to see the doctor. It's the usual thing. He's pretty straight and I'm not.

He tells me I made a decision to be mediocre. At some very early point in my life. He gives me Laing's *The Divided Self* to read. He tells me I have great capacity, that I don't have to be mediocre any more. He tells me I have a choice. I listen to him but my gut is telling me exactly what I really need. I need to dry out so I can get on with it.

Mental Status (cont'd):
    The patient cried but didn't seem sincere. No trace of real emotion. He lacks insight.

After lunch I have AA visitors. They're charming people, and much harder to avoid than the doctor. They're drunks, and they know my moves.

They offer me a recovery program. A six-month voluntary commitment. Lovely surroundings. One of the women went through the program herself. She looks at me in a way I'm not used to. She's looking at me and through me at the same time. I could be a pane of glass in her house that some kid scribbled on. Her kindness scares me. Anyway, I just need to dry out.

Two days later I'm detoxed. I slip the orderly a five to get my clothes cleaned and pressed. When he brings them back I hang them on the door and look at them for a minute.

My car is in the Reno car pound, my money is in the safe, my clothes are clean and hanging on the door. I'm full of enthusiasm. I won't drink. I decided this morning they're right. I'm not going to drink anymore.

I say goodbye to Henry. We shake hands and he asks me to tell his wife he's sorry. Rosemary is in her room having her legs wrapped. The walker is making his rounds.

Patricia, the nurse, tells me again I should be in a program. She doesn't really get it. I've already stopped.

Dr. Fabian gives me his copy of *The Divided Self.*

I call a cab, and on the way out to the parking lot I turn back and get to see Ward 6 from the outside. It's old, red brick, and long and high. It looks like an armory.

Crossing the grass I feel pretty damned good.

Psychodynamics:

Schizoid—a false front. He takes many in with his intelligence.

Guilty for those he's injured and believes this to be another result of his insincerity.

At the pound my car is waiting. It's a '65 Fury and the shocks and springs are gone. I hardly care. It gets the job done. Just like I do. When I have to. I feel tough, and resilient.

There's a cop at the pound who was there when they picked me up. He lets me know it right away. "You should be ashamed of yourself," he says, "the crap you put your mother through."

I'll head out to Tahoe and see my kids.

When I leave it's dark.

A nice, dark breeze is up and my hands are steady on the wheel. My new bottle is flat on the passenger seat. I can make anybody believe anything. God, I love my kids. So, insane in the dark with a cobweb of plans in my head and a fifth in the passenger seat, I hit the road. The plans have a sentimental shine to them. They open into a future the way the music that opens *Pinocchio* swells.

The orgiastic future.

The only trouble with living in the future is that you wake up one morning and the future is standing there with a back-alley smile on its face, and a lead pipe in its hand.

The past is just as bad. The past just hurts.

FIFTEEN

In my wallet, carefully folded, is the card Bridget sent me last Easter. "This is to certify that you are my father and that I love you very much," it says. Also, "signed, Bridget Erdmann."

I head back to Tahoe. I could be driving my car through the galaxy. I'm that alone. I stop once in the black pines by the side of the road. I piss and look out in the dark. Turning back, my car's headlights are beams in space. God has never said a word to me, and that's a fact.

Our house is very dark. I stop the car in the dirt driveway and go quietly up on the deck and around to the chairs in back. They're all asleep and I'm moving and alive in the dark. I'm a presence. I sit down facing away into the trees.

I didn't drink all that much in the car. The house is a three dimensional, wooden puzzle, and I'm a missing piece. When a breeze comes up I rearrange my legs and hit the bottle twice. It's a little like the steps in Mill Valley. I'm out here in the dark between them and the world.

I fall asleep in the hard chair but not for long. When I

wake up it's still dark. I didn't drop the bottle. The feelings I had before I passed out feel like something good I've done. I never have dreams. When I have to sleep it comes fast and I sink deeper than where they come from.

The thing now is to get back in the car and take care of business. My headlights catch a deer when I turn them on. I'm humming *Satin Doll*. By the time the black is lightening, I'll be a hundred miles from here. That's when I'll get some breakfast. The deer is posed in yellow light and so am I, in my own way.

Why I'd call my sister Pat in a blackout, I don't know. I do, though. I cry and tell her I'm going to die. Death isn't my fear, but when you try to explain it you use the words you think straight people will understand. It's not like Reno, I guess, because she doesn't have to send the police like Mom did. Death isn't anything. It's the fear. The fear hurts like nothing I've ever known.

A ticket to St. Louis is waiting for me at the airport. I try to get myself together for the cab ride. Airports are all right because they're full of bars. What I see takes place in a three-foot square cube in front of me.

On the plane they give me oxygen. There's a shifting blur of grey skirts. A doctor feels my pulse and listens to my heart and says, "This man is dying." The fuck I am. He puts me in a place where I can fight.

The plane is met by an ambulance and a priest. It takes me to the VA hospital. The oxygen mask is cool and light, and all I have to do is lie there and breathe. It feels pretty good. Mom's face is all around the edges of everything. There are drugs in the hospital. That's how I need to get dry. Three meals a day and drugs. A clean, white bed. When they take my clothes I notice the sores on my legs. I can handle that but when I start to throw up I'm filling the basin with blood. Christ. It's dark and slick and there's a lot of it. I'll have to do just what they tell me till I'm better. I'll be cheerful and pliant and I won't die.

I have no sense of humor and lightness eludes me. I'm a commando, trapped behind enemy lines.

Mom is still Marian. Her hair is all grey now but that's because she's older. That makes sense. Pat looks at me a little differently. I can feel her feeling things. I never could before. Her husband doesn't think much of me. He's polite enough, but I'm the guy on the coast who calls and makes his wife cry.

I'm staying with Mom. It's a two-bedroom apartment. Under my mattress is a pint of Gilbey's and downstairs, behind the dumpster in back, is a fifth of Wolfschmidt's. When I think of a drink the individual labels swim up in color. Mom doesn't know. What does Mom know?

We chat together about the kids, and Sara, and stuff from the old days she doesn't think will depress me. We don't talk about the divorce. Mom is into the Church now like a flower in an ornamental garden. The rest of the family shows little interest in seeing me. That's fine. I go out to the Post Office a lot.

"I think I'll walk down to the Post Office."

"Oh, Jack. Would you pick me up a book of stamps?"

Shit. It's out of my way.

If mom can't smell the alcohol she has no idea whether I've been drinking or not.

She has albums of photographs. We sit together and look at them delicately.

Three days later I'm in a motel in California, down on the peninsula. There's a knock at the door and I open it to a serious, younger man with glasses. "Hi, Jack," he says, "I'm from Suicide Prevention."

What the fuck. I've missed something again.

I let him in and we talk.

It's over, I tell him. I just got back from some heavy family stuff and I started a new job too and I guess I drank more than I could handle and let the depression get out of control. We talk about his work and it moves me deeply. I write him a donation check for $25 and ease him to the door. I better get the fuck out of here.

I need to stay away from the phone. I need to stop embarrassing myself. But I don't seem to be able to do it. I don't know what it is. The hospital helped. Drying out helped.

I head back toward the Golden Gate. I need a place to stay. The sun is shining and traffic is light. Suddenly it's twilight and I get myself a motel room.

I'll lie completely on my ass and watch the television.

Remember that Nat King Cole record of *Red Sails in the Sunset?* God, I loved that. What saves me is that I really like to be alone. If I didn't, I'd have a hard time. I remember some of my happiest times in that old garage across the alley. Somebody or other's. Some old lady. It felt like a teepee and I could just sneak in and sit there by myself. I was real young too. I always had a taste for it.

I slip and fall on an ice cube on my way to the bathroom. No damage. I'll have some bourbon tonight. I don't drink bourbon that much anymore. But dark liquor seems to put me to sleep better than light liquor. I want to get a good night's sleep. The movie at two is *Letter From An Unknown Woman.* It's pretty good. It makes me cry.

I don't mind crying at good movies when I'm alone. I knock my glass over reaching for the bottle. I move over to the other side of the bed so that when I wake up I don't jump out on the broken glass. I don't have to get up in the morning. The movie is over at four.

I feel pretty bad in the morning. The phone is off the hook and making that terrible noise. The difference between my

father and me is that he was a weakling and I'm not. I don't
sit in my chair and cry. I don't terrify children.

I get up and get dressed and start to bend over to clean
up the glass. No, no, maybe later. I have to drive that car
across the freeway to the Strawberry Shopping Center.
There's a liquor store. There are beads of sweat on my forehead and I'm doing everything very slowly. I need to find a
current to move in, but that's not how the traffic is. It seems
to take me a very long time. Black and white are colors I'm
aware of.

In the liquor store I pick up two fifths of vodka and give
the guy a check. He looks at the check for a long time. I
know it's good. He says he'll be right back and goes to the
glassy back of the store. He comes back and he puts one
hand on the top of my bag on the counter. "Sorry, Mr.
Erdmann. It's just that we're having a lot of trouble with bad
checks lately. It'll be just a minute while we run it through
the machine."

It's taking a long time and I can taste the liquor through
the brown paper. My knees are starting to shake. He wants
to talk about the weather. He asks me about the Giants.

"Danger," my head says.

I grab the bag and head to the door as fast as I can. The
phone was off the hook. The goddamn phone was off the
hook. In the parking lot a black-and-white is coming over
the empty black-top like it's glass. The red light is glowing
and flashing.

It's an APB. I called Pat again and she called the police.
They take me to the Marin County Crisis Center. There
are guys with bandaged wrists. Depressed and drugged and
isolate. There's a girl who *knows* an intruder has killed her
whole family in the night. A staff member says, "Hey, Carol,
been talking to God lately?" The walls are neutral and none

of the pool table cues have tips on them. There are volunteers and continual typing. The orderlies look like bouncers.

Three days later I see a psychiatrist. He asks me two or three stupid questions and lets me go. I take a cab back to my car. I go to Tahoe.

I get as far as the River Ranch in Alpine Meadows. The river-rafters go there. It's rustic, and the Truckee is right outside. In the twilight the sound of the river goes by in sculpted burbles. I sit at the bar and know my room is only twenty feet away. At night the river is louder. The Truckee is an old friend, and I think I'm going to sleep right tonight. Sometimes that happens.

Next day I eat some breakfast. I sit on the deck and watch the river. I've missed too many days. It seems like I miss the days and all my nerves are sharp and aware at twilight.

By noon I need to lie down. I go to my room but even with the curtains drawn there's too much light coming in. I go back to the bar and pick up a double. I wander out to the end of the wooden walkway where the walkway and the parking lot come together on the high edge of the river. I slide on the loose stones and fall ten feet into the water. I hit my head on the rocks. The fall is like one of those movements in your sleep that jar you awake, scared.

In the hospital I'm very quiet. I say thank you to the nurses. I explain to the doctor yes, I'd been drinking. Yes, I know I have a problem and it's time to do something about it.

A couple comes to see me from the Open Door Detox. They're so kind to me. I feel like I've never done anything for anyone else in my entire life. I haven't. I'm not worth their time. They're so motherfucking kind. A word like kind is suddenly different. It means something.

They'll take me to the Detox. I can't stop crying.

Something is broken, and I'm not worth their time.

When you're detoxing your nerves are like a loose sheet

somebody's thrown over you. It's like the air is fear, and the room is fear, and the bed, most of all, is fear. You have to stay as still as you can so you don't stir it up. Like a dream, always like a dream. The dream they're looking for you in. You know you're not really hidden but hold very still and hope they don't notice.

Everybody's kind, but I can't really hear them. My feeling is that they're misguided. I can't fault them, but they just don't know me.

When I leave, detoxed, one of the staff guys gives me his card. It's for the police. He says, "If you get in trouble, Jack, give them this."

Send Jack to me, is written across it.

"Thanks, Ray. I won't need it, but thanks."

I get back on the road for Marin. Next to the phone booth is a slot machine. I put a quarter in and hit a $250 jackpot. The machine whistles and rings and soon there's a small crowd around me. $250 is no big deal and I don't know why I draw a crowd. They look at me but look away when I look back. I turn to the bar and the mirror.

I didn't know. I was in the Detox for four days and I never really saw my face. I mean, I knew I had a bruise and a lump but I never *saw* it. Not like this. There were mirrors in the bathroom. How did I not know? How did I get like this?

The right side of my forehead is a half grapefruit. It's the worst swelling I've ever seen. It's the worst swelling they've ever seen. I head to the bathroom and cry over the sink.

They think this is me. They think this is what I really look like.

I get a double and an off-sale fifth.

"Jeez," the bartender says, "did a job on yourself, huh?"

"Took a fall. It's not as bad as it looks."

"Jeez, I hope not."

I'm jagged and raw and crazy, and I punch the car back

to Marin. At twilight I get a room. I have most of the bottle left. In the morning the lump is still there. I go out to a liquor store where they don't know me, pick up a new supply, and sneak back into my room.

I'm in my room for three days. On the morning of the third day it crosses my mind that the kids have a drunk for a mother and a suicide for a father. I've been lying on the bed for a couple of hours trying to saw through my wrist with a cartridge razor blade. It doesn't feel like the morning. I know it's silly but I don't think I can get up. I know I can't get to a store. A suicide for a father. They're so small and trusting. They were so small. I crawl down the hall to the living room and come to in Novato General Hospital.

Who knows who these people are? I have to make an effort to talk to them, to bridge the gap. They have their professional masks, and I have mine.

In the dark I can't see anything but there are low voices coming toward me. A flashlight clicks on my face and a woman's voice says, "See that? That's where you're going. Is that where you want to go?"

"Jesus," a man's voice says.

I'm in Lincoln House in the upstairs bedroom. I can almost remember. Lincoln House is the San Rafael detox. It's not medical. Drunks helping other drunks.

In the morning I met Tom Kay. With sandy hair and very observant eyes. I'm sunk in a big, black chair. Tom's friend, Mike the Electrician, comes in and says, "Jack the Lump. That's what we'll call him, Jack the Lump." Tom laughs and I try to smile.

I'm trying now. I really am. They take me to meetings and I listen. But I know that somehow my problems are different. I'm alone in the middle of a room full of drunks. I'm so scared of the street. I'm so scared of it that the fear itself will drive me back out for a bottle to kill it with.

In the Emergency Room I'm on a gurney and a nurse with a perfect woman's voice bends down and says in my ear, "We're not going to let you go today, Jack. You're not going to die." It's a marvelous thing to say. For the weight of the gesture. The message means very little.

In the Crisis Center I'm out of control. They throw me in the padded cell. The one dim bulb is way up and purplish on the green walls. I'm a purely frightened animal. I'm a horse in a fire. When they get tired of my noise two orderlies come in. One of them sits on my chest and methodically beats the shit out of me.

"How's that? You like that?"

When I'm quiet they tie me down on the bed. My wrists are looped and I try to pop my hands off their ends. When they let me up I stay very calm and look for a way out.

I find an empty office with a window. The window opens out at its top. I can get half my body out, but my head won't go. I've lost about thirty-five pounds but my head is the same size. Bigger with what's left of the lump. I get stuck and I stay there quietly till they find me.

They want to send me to Napa but the people at Lincoln House say no, send him back to us.

Tom talks to me a lot. And Irv. There are people trying to help me everywhere. Sometimes I'm sober for as long as two weeks. If I can just keep the *presence* of the sober time while mixing the liquor in slowly. So I hit a balance point. So I can be sober, really, but keep the fear down with the alcohol. I'll go to Steve.

He's across a big, wide street. I'm parked in front of Colonial Liquors and Steve's place, from the number, has to be on the other side. There's a big turn in the road and the traffic comes swooping around it blind. I pick up a pint and I stand with my finger on the "Press Button To Cross" button. I hurry when the light changes. My steps don't cover enough ground for me to feel safe.

Steve's is a basement studio. It's right across the street from the Colonial. He opens the door and says, "Hi, Dad," and stands back to let me come in. The door is that wavy glass you see in credit offices, and the apartment is small and square. There's only one window at the street end. A door is blocked up to serve as a table. His clarinet is out by a music stand.

"How's it going kid?"

"Pretty good."

"I need to ask you a favor."

"Yeah."

"I lost my apartment and I need a place to stay till I find something else."

"Yeah."

"What do you think?"

"I don't know, Dad, it's small."

"I won't be here all that much. I'll just put a pad on the floor in the corner."

"I guess."

"I'm not drinking. You don't have to worry about that. The doctor told me I'd *have* to stop."

"That's great."

"Yeah."

Steve is studying music at the College of Marin. He works washing dishes in a local restaurant. I hide my bottles, mostly outside in the trees and shrubbery on the side of the steep driveway. I try to stay out of the apartment till late. Every night I get us a six-pack before we go to sleep. I need it to sleep, and it's just beer. Steve drinks a few and doesn't seem to mind.

The cars in the road make a terrific noise. During the rush hour you can't even hear the television. We have a little kitchen. When someone passes down the hall his shadow ripples across the glass on our door. The light in the hall is always on. I have a fifth between my mattress and the wall. It's stuffed in a high sock so it won't clank. I have a fifth under the tree outside and a pint pushed down behind the battery in the car.

I figure he doesn't know I'm drinking. But if he does, that's all right, too, because he isn't saying anything about it, and that's the important part. I chew up the breath mints, hold them in my mouth and breathe in formally and deeply. I hold them in the back of my throat and let the liquid trickle down slowly. I stay there most of the time. When Steve's out. I take off before he comes back and walk in a couple of hours later. I've been out on business.

I don't remember a lot. When the twilight comes it's like I just woke up. Mom calls in tears. I've been calling her again. I know I woke up in the drunk tank and the police told me I'd been wedged in the phone booth in the Colonial parking lot. The receiver was dangling and the fire department had to come to get me out. I'd been crying and screaming at a poor woman as if I were newly born and still covered with blood.

I'm lying there and I can hear my own nose making noises. I'm not quite asleep and headlights are cutting bright rectangles across the ceiling. Steve is in bed too. I hear him get up and he starts to play a bluesy clarinet, very softly.

"Son-of-a-bitch. You think you could let me get some sleep?"

"I thought you were asleep."

"I'm not fucking asleep and I don't need any fucking clarinet to keep me awake."

I get up. He's on his feet too.

"Shut up, Dad."

"You're a fucking asshole, you know that? You're a fucking prick asshole. A fucking inconsiderate asshole."

His face is in parts from the different half-lights.

"Damn you, goddamn you."

"Sad-sack jerk-off with a jerk-off clarinet."

He hits me and knocks me back on my mattress. He jumps on my chest and his fingers lock around my throat. He's choking me and I'm just lying there. He stops. Without his glasses his eyes are hot.

"Get the fuck out of here."

I get out and grab my pint from behind the battery. I drive away.

It's light out and my head is on the steering wheel. I'm in a shopping center parking lot by the freeway. There's a woman's face at the driver's side window. I've just come from the funeral parlor. I remember Steve laid out in the dimness with his hands folded and his glasses on. He died of an overdose.

"Is there anything I can do? Are you all right?"

"My son is dead."

"Oh, God, I'm sorry. Can I do anything? Is there anyone I can call?"

I'm crying from way down. My face and hands are completely wet.

"It's just my son is dead."

"I'm so sorry. Will you be all right here?"

"Not anywhere."

The apartment is empty, and noisy with cars. My bottle is in the sock. I sit down on the mattress across from the table and the music stand.

It's very dark and I feel particularly cold. I'm outside. I raise up my hands and hold them in front of me. They're bloody and the nails are broken. I'm digging at the root of the pine for where I hid the other bottle. I'm crouched in the driveway in my underwear, and cars are going by in the street. I see my hands very clearly and a voice in my head says "You need help," just before I go under again.

I called up Duffy's in Calistoga. It's a recovery house. I'm in the phone booth by the Colonial, and I'm waiting for a cab. I have the last of the last money my mother sent. I'm going to Duffy's. I get in the cab and half-lie down, bent at the waist. My beautiful son is dead. I send the driver in to get a bottle. I tell him I need it or I'll be sick in the cab. It's a long drive.

All I can see is the sky.

I'm in a doorway and my feet are dragging behind me. The tips of my shoes. There are hands under my arms and they're hurting me. There are people watching me through the door. This is bullshit.

"I can walk," I say.

I shrug off the hands and put one foot over the sill. I go down in a very soft heap. It doesn't hurt at all. I can't feel a thing.

What could I say anyway? "Hey, Mom, Jack's home?"

SIXTEEN

When you finally get to the bottom of your personality there isn't anything there. You're on the open train station, what's left of you when your personality is gone.

If you know what it's like to wake up in the dark and not know where you are, that's what it's like. At the bottom of your personality it's just like that. None of the past means anything. The part of you that isn't your body and shaking is your soul. You can feel it like you can feel the hole in your chest and the organs in it. It's just there.

In the hallway at Duffy's there are photographs on the wall. I think they're photographs. There's a whir down the hall where the kitchen is. Ernie's in the kitchen under the fluorescent lights. He's mostly a face with eyes.

"Damn, you look bad. Sit down. Sit down here and stay here. I'll be right back. You hear me?"

There isn't any way to move. My forearms are down on my thighs and I'm bent off the chair but not too much. I don't want to look up because the light is wrong. It's the hell-light, with the stainless steel and the white and the dangerous machines. All machines are dangerous. Blocks are placed on the floors to catch my feet. In the simplest things there are difficulties most people never see. It's like I'm a technical illustration of how physical forces interact. There are lines of force and vectors and blocking steel. There's a fear that the world will always be flat. The Fear of How Things Move. I Am Still Alive.

My hands hang off my thighs. They're filling up with blood. I can feel that. My blood isn't moving fast enough and it's collecting in the ends of my body. I rest my elbows on my thighs with my hands straight up. Ernie's coming back with a hummer. A hummer is a drink they give you periodically to get you through the worst. He's in the doorway.

I'm in a vacuum and the only thing that will keep the world from rushing into me is a drink. There's a bright green toothbrush sticking out of the far wall. I have to stop looking at it. God, I didn't want to do this. I'm not anything, I'm just a thing. And I never wanted to do this and I'm sorry but the kitchen doesn't want to hear about it and neither does God, who's outside of this, and the only thing outside that's moving away from me. God, I think, is moving away from me.

The tracks in the back at Winona St. were shiny because they were used all the time. In yellow grass and weeds and junk you'd expect them to be rusted. But they were shiny when you got up close. I can't do anything now but if I wait I'll be able to do things and if I think clearly, and stay straight for a while, I'll be able to kill myself right. Ernie's in front of me but I don't want to look into his eyes. I want to look at the drink before I take it. "Here, man," he says, and puts it out right in front of my chest. It's as amber as the light isn't, and I drink it in an easy, open-throat gulp.

"Thank you."

I'm not looking at him. I'm looking at the toothbrush. It's

not that I couldn't look at him, it's just that I'd have to tip my head back to do it and that seems like something I'd rather not do. The drink isn't doing a hell of a lot. I need a pint. It takes out the edge very slightly, with a slight eraser-shadow.

"How long is it now?"

"Three days."

"I was talking to somebody."

"That was Ali. She sees you a lot."

"I think I was blacked-out."

"Blacked-out doesn't cover it, man."

I remember she's sitting at the edge of my bed when I wake up. It's a small room with a window and the shade down. "Where are you, Jack?"

"I know where I am."

"Where's that?"

"I'm in a flop-house in Philadelphia."

"Have you ever been in Philadelphia?"

"No."

This is confusing, like most black-out wake-ups. I've never been in Philadelphia. I'm not in Philadelphia. It's probably a hospital. I'm probably in a mental hospital. Reno? San Francisco? It's not the Crisis Center, the room is too much like a room. It's not Lincoln House. The woman has blue eyes. When I look at her eyes it's like I'm looking at me but I'm not there. I'm Jack Erdmann. She makes me cry. Ernie does too. I have big, shapeless tears gathering at the rims of my eyes. I don't blink so they won't roll down. I don't want them to know, I think. This time I don't want anybody to know where I am. Steve is dead and I'm dead, and that's where I'm going to stay. Nobody notices what it's like to be alive. That's why they walk around that way. You're always touching something. Now I don't care. I don't have to care. I don't have to move without thinking about it first. It's very important. I know that. If I don't move without planning-it-out, I won't break. It took a lot to move at all and I'm not going to lose it now.

"You all right?"

"Could I just sit here?"

"You can sit wherever you like, but look, if you get scared you tell me. You tell me right away. When you start to get scared is when you seize-up. Now there's no reason for that to happen. You hear me? No reason to be scared. We're all with you. Nobody here ain't been through it."

"I killed my son."

"You didn't kill no one that I know about. You don't want to be listening to your head. That's how you got here. You listened to your head. Now you can just can that shit. You're safe here. You *know* that. Now pay attention."

When I get my strength back. When I can do what I want. When I get outside it'll all be there. I'll do all the same things. It doesn't matter. I'm safe here. Take it for what it's worth. I'm alone in the dark but they think they're with me. Do what you're told, Jack. For Christ's sake, do what you're told.

There's a terrible, pale light coming up at the windows. The dawn is worse than the twilight. With help I get back to my room. It's darker there. I know it's possible to believe something and not believe it at the same time. In the heavy-draped room at Keaton's Mortuary, Steve is laid out with his high-lit glasses on. The drapes are as heavy as my grand-mother's drapes, and there's a man right behind me with his hands folded. He's not saying anything because he respects my grief. I've *been* there. But I don't really believe there's a green toothbrush coming out of the wall in the kitchen, and Ernie says Steve isn't dead. What does Ernie know? He knows whatever comes through the office. He knows what's in my file. I must have a file. What difference does it make right now. If Steve is dead, well, I'm dead too. I didn't kill him, that's just how it feels. I killed my father too, for that matter. We could all just hold hands and forget it happened. At any time we could all have just stopped and said, "Well, that's enough for that game. Let's do something else." Why didn't we do that? I never thought about it, that I killed my father. Steve, I guess, wanted to kill me. But he didn't. And we all probably loved each other. I don't know what Dad was feeling. He must have been at least as scared as me. More. The way his neck collapsed like there wasn't any spine anymore and his head could only lie there while I held it in my arms like a melon. The Virgin Mary is very pretty in her blue robes.

It doesn't matter now. It doesn't matter now. It doesn't matter now.

Every time I wake up there's somebody in the room with me. I'm starting to wake up for good. That's when you shake and you don't sleep. Coming back when they expect you to *do* things. I don't want to do anything. Gene Duffy's voice comes booming out of the speaker. I pick up the syllables but the only real information I'm getting is coming out of the alive eyes in my room.

Ali is pretty and lively. She loves to talk and sits with me for hours. Death row is where I am. When I'm a little better, I'll get to move. No one can help me but me, they all tell me that. But secretly and helplessly I suck on their eyes like a wounded vampire. A wounded vampire sucking at human kindness. Herb is the guy who got me out of the cab. He has a weathered face. He's an alcoholic and speed-freak. Duffy let him stay and work past his allotted time. The shock of human kindness is all over him.

"You don't have to do it any more, man. You already hit your bottom. You can't go any lower, man, all you can do is die and that's just bullshit." That's what it is. But it's bullshit, too, to be lying here like a sick kid with weak fingers on the edge of a blanket. I feel like a leaf. I can think of a lot of things I feel like. It doesn't matter now.

I make my first appearance in the big front room. It's dark outside. I get down the hall not too bad, with one hand on the wall, but when I get to the end of the hall I trip slightly and it's like some other force throws me through the entrance. It's like a surface dive from the edge of a pool. I land on my nose and my chest and someone says, "Way to go, Jack." They take me back to my room and a very sensitive Black man talks my heart back down.

If I don't make it I can always kill myself. Now there's a certainty. I hold on to it when the images start to take over. I thought of it the first night and it got me through to the morning. I'll think of it tonight and it will get me through to tomorrow.

Steve called. Ali tells me that. I'm sure Ali wouldn't lie to me so I'm sure Steve isn't dead. I feel pretty certain that no one is lying to me. It's not an ordinary feeling. But I've come too far. If Steve isn't dead then I killed him in my head. Why would I do that? It won't kill you, they tell me. It only feels like it can. You have nothing you can do, there's no way to live your life anymore because nothing works. You're just afraid.

I can be dead anytime I want to. Almost anytime. I'm not together enough yet to bring it off and anyway, they don't let me have anything I could do it with.

We say the Lord's Prayer. We join hands after meetings and pray. The way I shake it's terrible to reach out on each side for someone else's hand. I jerk and vibrate and twitch. I feel like I'm shaking the whole circle. The hell with God. God left me alone when I was a boy and now he's backing away. They tell me I need a higher power. Outside and across the field is a steep and rounded, rocky hill. That's my higher power. I look at it with a kind of disinterested hope. I take it all in. Alcohol has rejected me, and when I go back out on the street where alcohol rules, I'll need the precise outlines of this precise hill. One guy tells me he uses the doorknob on the front door as his higher power. A lot of drunks have trouble with God, trouble with even the word.

There are slogans everywhere. The slogans I thought were simple-minded when Tom used to take me to meetings. One Day At A Time. Keep It Simple. They aren't simple at all. Nothing is simple. But Ali says they are. Simple, but not easy.

When I was a boy I needed to get away. Well who the fuck wouldn't? If the priests are really God's priests we're in bad trouble. My hill is green and beige with flat grey faces in it.

There's a long porch with a row of chairs on it. Over it is a trellised arbor and out in front four paths converge on a circle of five young cedars. The porch is where it's going on. For me anyway. We sit out there in the sunlight and talk it over. We try not to lie. It's a rare place. I think about it and I can't ever remember being with two or more people who were trying not to lie. It's a particular and special experience. "If I can make it, anyone can make it." Everyone says that, sooner or later.

I'm not allowed to make phone calls. I think it'll kill me. I need to make everything all right. I need to get on the phone and tell everyone that everything's going to be all right. Everything I ever did is coming back in waves. I can't stop it anymore. Steve is always eight years old and leading his brother and sister up the stairs in the house in Mill Valley. His head comes slowly up the stairs in my head with an absolute, plug-pulling certainty. I lost him in the dark I swore he'd never know about. Please help me. It doesn't matter right now.

Alcohol rules the street. It's no joke. Liquor stores, bars, restaurants, grocery stores, and billboards, like on 17 in the east bay where huge images of sex and comfort and cheap liquor snap by like riffled cards. My second level of sickness is coming in. I'm so goddamned afraid that I won't make it that I can taste the first swallow and inside the fear of it, the conviction that once I take it I won't be afraid anymore and the future will back off just like it used to.

And the past, Jesus, I need to be free so fuck the past. I have a disease, okay, I'll buy that because my father had it too, and I come by it honestly. But it's my disease. And it's my pain. And if anybody doesn't like what I do with it, that's too damn bad. I *know* it's out there and I'm powerless. It's so fucking complicated. Nothing can be put right anyway.

Please help me.

I ask my hill.

And Ali. I go to her office and knock. I'm rehearsing what to say in my head. I don't want anyone to be angry at me.

"I need a drink," I say.

"What a surprise."

"I can't stand it. I need to go out and get a drink."

"You *want* to go out and get a drink."

"I'm fucking scared."

"I know, Jack. What do you think you can do about it?"

"I need you to sit on my chest till it passes."

"God, Jack, is this a proposition?"

"No."

My sense of humor is gone.

"Go get us some coffee."

She talks to me for hours, about everything. When I go back to my room I'm only there for five minutes before there's a knock on the door. It's Herb. When Herb leaves, Paul comes by. And Jeff and Kenny and Dave. They talk me through to dinner time. After dinner there's a meeting.

"It's a gift," the speaker says. "I asked for it and the faith came in."

Maybe I'm asking wrong.

I wish I had my music. Getz's *Skylark*, Hawkins' *Body and Soul*. I wish to God I were someone else and nobody knew me. My coins and stamps are still in my car. Wherever my car is. The things I carried around. I wanted them to be important. None of them were. I wanted something to be real.

Real-Life, Real-Life. What do you do when you don't drink? There's all the time going by. There's nothing to do but think about the future and the future is going to be just like sitting around thinking about the future. I see myself back in some furnished room in somebody's house. It's two in the afternoon and I'm sitting there. That's the day. It's x o'clock and I'm sitting there. God. I'm going to have to leave here and I am scared.

Ernie's around at night. When I can't sleep I talk to him.

"Look at it, Jack. When you came in here you was almost dead. Now you're not. When you came in here you was drunk. Now you're not. Right now you're scared, but tomorrow you won't be. You want a drink tomorrow, there's all the booze in the world right down the block. It ain't goin' nowhere."

I can get a job somewhere else. Somewhere different, things will be different.

"The trouble with a drunk on a geographic is he brings himself along."

I need some time alone to think.

"When you're alone you're in bad company."

Alcohol is my best friend.

"It chewed you up and it spit you out. You're on your own."

I stand in the doorway to my room. There's a moon tonight and it's not very dark. I'm willing to be willing. That's important. It's all I've got going for me. "Fake it 'til you make it." I hear that a lot. I'm sick and crazy and my higher power is a hill in Calistoga. There's one thing I think I've learned on my own. The images come out of the front of my head. When they start to dance and close in, I can feel them peeling themselves off the brain behind my forehead like decals. When the images dance the fear is all over everything like a tacky, glutinous film.

There's a voice in the back of my head, though. It doesn't deal in images and when I can hear it, not all the time, it tells me things with a quiet certainty.

That's where I try to say, "Please help me." I try to vibrate the words in a triangle way in the back of my head. It's my prayer. I don't know what else to say. This time I kneel. It makes me feel foolish.

Herb takes me up to the top floor in the old red barn. There are stacks of boxes of clothes. The clothes I'm wearing, they found around the main house. They're about eight sizes too big. Everything about me flops. The soles on my loafers are semi-detached from missing curbs. They gape like cartoon mouths and make slapping noises. All the clothes in the barn were left behind by guys who ran. Lots of them. It's a very cold, factual place. It's like I heard a speaker say, "This isn't theory, this is what works. There's a pile of corpses eight miles high went into making this program."

It's good to have clothes that fit. This is the fifth day. I've only got three weeks.

We have groups in the morning. I'm very serious. With every passing hour I'm closer to having to go back outside. I'm rummaging around in what I hear for that one piece of shining information that'll make it possible for me never to go back to where I was. I can't go back there. I never find it, and in the groups and the tapes and the meetings "spiritual" is the word that comes to grate on me, like what? Something bad. My head is a leveled city where every brick has been separated from every other brick. "The things you thought you knew were wrong. Let go." I've *been* spiritual. I put in my time on a narrow, adolescent bed. I've wheedled, cajoled and threatened God, and all I've got to show for it is a stamp collection, a wounded family and a head full of spiders. Fuck God.

Nothing happens.

I remember the kind of peace I used to get at the bar. Way back, the bar in St. Louis, the solid peace that came up out of my belly. I could see it in the mirror. My tongue would move and words would come easy, and sketch-me-out in the air. It *was* spiritual. Alcohol is the closest I've ever gotten to the spiritual, and now they're telling me I need it if I want to save my ass. I've prayed to my hill but I'll be goddamned if I'm going to pray to the God of the Catholic Church. Nobody's really asking me to. I've got to sort that out. There's a tangle. And it's killing me.

Ali is walking down the hall in front of me and she looks good. Why am I lusting after a woman when I doubt I can even get it up? Lust for when I can again. No. Lust in my head that has nothing to do with my body. There is a gap. There's a space between my head and my belly. I remember I ate too many novocaine throat lozenges once and I thought I could feel my stomach getting numb. She opens her door and goes into her office. I like to think she knew I was watching. I like to think.

The way I remember it, when I first started talking to Dad while he cried, I believed what I was telling him. I wasn't really sure, but in the instant, trying to make him stop and make him love me at the same time, I believed. I'm going to cry again and the front room is full. I wander out the door. He didn't know who I was. I was sitting there hidden in the music and he had no idea. Whatever the fuck he knew or didn't know, it isn't important now. It doesn't matter now.

Forgive me father, for I have sinned. God is not my father. My father wasn't God. I hope, at least, that I know that. I turn the corner of the main building and look at my hill. This is getting silly. The Hill of My Fathers' with stones in it.

I know I'm drinking too much coffee, but Jesus, you can't give up everything. I put too much sugar in it, too. The sugar seems to calm me.

One of my new talents is standing very still for long periods of time. It's physical. I don't want to do anything sudden, so I stay very still. The colors back here are simple and light. It's a good place to stand, in the middle of the simple. A car is coming up the driveway. It's another cab.

The guy who gets out is moving real slow. He's trying to frown. In blue work shirt and jeans he's trying to look like a hard-guy. He has a suitcase and one of the latches is open. The guys on the porch are watching with interest. He gets half way up the stairs before he slips and falls with the tips of his boots skipping down the stairs. The suitcase breaks open and it's all gone, everything he wanted to be.

"Motherfucker," he says, and two guys from the porch go down to help him up. Except for me, they're just about the physically sickest in the place. They help him with a lot of delicacy. One of them shakes as he tries to get the suitcase latched.

"It's okay, brother, you're in the right place."

For me, the whole thing is in slow motion. There's something here. It's like in a shaking sick man bending down to put together another sick man's belongings you can see the effort he's making to save himself.

Compassion is the measure of how much he wants to save himself. It's a delicate, fluttery instant.

"If I can make it, anybody can."

There is something here. Okay.

I hear about lives that have been so much worse than mine it embarrasses me. But there's a curious thing. The pain all seems the same. There doesn't seem to be any hierarchy. The pain is independent of events. That's what they mean by a spiritual sickness. Every time I recognize a meaning it's like the easing of a cramp. For a little while, I'm going to feel pretty good. I'm happy with my mind for doing its job. There's not much chance that will last.

"You got here by listening to your head."

It's after lunch and the big front room is mostly empty. It feels like a goddamn hunting lodge, or a roadhouse. It has the big fireplace and the dark wood, and the walls are covered with signed photographs.

A tape is playing over the PA system. Duffy is good: tough and accurate. But I'm not really listening. I've got my hands between my knees in a down-bent prayer-clasp. I hold them there because it keeps them from flying around. I'm bent and curved into the couch and I wonder if I'll ever get over the shakes. My head is down and I'm not hearing anything but the rustle in my head as the blood goes through.

". . . . God could and would if He were sought."

The words get in.

It's not just my head. My head is what hears them but something else takes them in, and they open in my belly and chest like stop-motion flowers. I know that something true has gotten inside. He can and He will. I never have to feel that way again. He can and He will. I'm amazed at myself. This is what grace is like. This is food, and it was hanging in the air. I'm on the couch and I can't remember what I'm afraid of. I can't remember what it feels like to be afraid. I'm out of excuses and the air is full.

I go in to see Duffy.

"Uh, Gene? You know that tape that was just on?"

"You might say that."

"The last part, the last words, what were they again?"

"Jesus, Erdmann. You know what you hear at meetings? Every goddamn night before the meetings?"

His voice gets louder.

"A. That we were alcoholic and could not manage our own lives. B. That probably no human power could have relieved our alcoholism. *"C.!"* he roars, *"That God Could And Would If He Were Sought!"*

"Yeah, that's it. Thanks Gene."

"Goddamn, Erdmann. Wake up."

This isn't the way it happens for everybody. I know that. Sometimes it just comes in and sometimes it grows slowly. It's not like everything is going to be easy, but it doesn't matter because I know what to do and I know where the strength to do it comes from.

God as I understand Him. I never really heard that either. God as I feel Him. I was right in one thing anyway. It is one foot in front of the other.

The compassion of the helpless.

SEVENTEEN

But there's always the street, then, to get along in the world.

It's like I came to this place because I didn't have anywhere else to go and I goddamn never did, really, I really never did. I thought I was okay and I never wanted to be like this. But I was a kid then and I got confused and I didn't know what to do. So here I am and I can't fucking stand it with the dark in my head and knowing how to fix it. Cross the street to Colonial Liquors where they know me and the building is white and clean with bottles on the shelves with glossy labels and liquids for the nerves the heart the dark the feet trying to walk the fear.

They know who I am. That makes me comfortable. When I pick up the bag it'll weigh just right and being scared will be over. I'll make my own space like a little bed that's goddamned well mine. And when I twist the top off the bottle my heart will sing like the music I used to hear when everything was okay.

And when I take a drink it'll blossom in my head and my throat will be warm and my feet will fit on the ground again.

And there'll be more in the bottle, anytime I want it. I can make it happen again and again. Maybe it isn't as good as it was but it's okay. The neat white store is right across the street. I could lie down and the bottle would be next to me.

I don't have to fucking feel like this. I'll wrap my nerves up and be like I was. I'm scared like I'm a kid and the people I thought I knew are shrieking with their faces changed and I'm looking up knowing there's nowhere for me to go. This is it kid. This is it, get used to it, figure it out, make something air-tight, protect yourself.

I'm forty-five years old and I have to go into where I live through a window down on the ground. I live in a basement apartment and I don't have the key anymore. I haven't had a drink in three weeks. My nerves are dying, screaming. Everything down there is dark and a horror and I have to go in and people will see me lying here wriggling with my ass in the air through a basement window like some fucking comic. Like Jack Lemmon. That's more like it, not funny just screaming and screaming and clawing the ground.

Behind me the traffic goes by on the four lane street; it's hard to cross. Across the street's the white front of Colonial Liquors. Four wide lanes and the cars come around the big turn toward the hospital going fast. Thwap they'll hit me stumbling, breaking and twisting and the road sliding on the side of my face. I can feel my head run over like a grapefruit. I can really feel it. I take a deep breath and get down on my knees by the window.

I have all this past and time invested in me. My mother did her best. My father crazy and drunk did his best too. They stuck him in the fucking sanitarium and treated him like meat. The drunks at Duffy's, their time. My sister, my wife, my kids—a shock there like a razor dragging on the front of my head. They want me to be someone else but I am not someone else. This is me.

They *know me* at the Colonial. I'm a pretty nice guy. I'm a fucking salesman and I can fake it. They have shelves and shelves of me, of the real me—when I'm feeling good and I'm taking care of things and I'm a hell of a nice guy. Ask anyone. I don't cry in my fucking beer. I'm one of the guys and I'm crawling through a basement window on my belly like a snake.

At Duffy's they told me when I'm alone I'm in bad company. Why should I be alone? Nobody wants me to be alone. When I call Mom she cries. She doesn't want me to be alone. It's not like Dad didn't try. My kids like me. They know who I really am. They'll always know. The window frame sticks so I break it with my forearm.

I wouldn't have stopped if I didn't have to. So I had to and I know it. BUT I'M NOT GOING TO MAKE IT BECAUSE I CANNOT FEEL LIKE THIS.

I can't. These are the feelings and I can't feel them when I'm well but I am not well and I will not feel them now because they'll kill me. Like my chest caving in. Like water through a drainpipe.

They told me all the stuff at Duffy's but here I am and the world is all around me full of blank faces and liquor stores. What the fuck is this? Do junkies come out and have to walk past billboards of elegant women with syringes? Do they advertise opiates on television?

I know what I should know and I'll go to meetings. I took the first step but sweet Jesus how can I do this. "My life had become unmanageable." Well yeah. Well no. No. My life had *never* been manageable. I was an alcoholic from the time I figured out how I didn't want to feel. That was a long time ago.

"I am powerless over alcohol." You see what the problem here is, *alcohol gave me the only power I had,* then took it away. The truth is I don't have anything left to manage. I have seven hundred pounds of fear, a locked door, and a liquor store across the street to manage. Power isn't real. You find that out.

Fear is real.

With the window broken open I can smell the apartment again. It smells like I did when I made it to Duffy's. I don't want to go in but I wriggle and snake and slide down the inside wall till my head stops me. At least it stops on the bed not the floor. My oldest son's bed is against the other wall. I tell myself he isn't dead. He isn't dead.

I told them he was, at Duffy's, I told the other drunks he was. It was a dream. I wasn't asleep, I just dreamed the trip to Keaton's Mortuary and Steve laid out in a suit with the room empty, just me and the shine off his glasses and these purple flowers. He looked so young I started to cry. I sat in my ludicrous van in the fucking imaginary parking lot and sobbed like my head was made of water. It was all a dream. I dreamed a lot of things.

So I start to cry again, feet still on the windowsill, face in the old mattress.

I get my feet down and lean with my back on the wall. It's dark. It's a long room like a coffin with some faint white at the end from the kitchen stuff. I get up and go to the refrigerator. There's a pint of vodka in the freezer and I stand there looking at it. Screaming and clawing the ground for a drink and the drink had been right in the freezer. I look at the advertising layout frost on the sides of the bottle. I look at everything I ever wanted. It felt so good then, when I first found out that alcohol made me clean and shiny and *lovable*.

I close the door and go way back down the room to the other end. I put my hands in my pockets.

I wish Steve were here and I'd tell him I love him. He'd know it's true because I'm sober. I think it should work that way. I need to get this stuff out of the way fast. So I won't hurt. So I can think about not drinking.

I have a phone so I need to call someone. I could call Duffy's but I just got out and I don't want them to know how scared I am. That's stupid because they already know how scared I am. No they don't, they don't know about this. This is not your average case. Yes it fucking is. Yes it is.

1. I am powerless over alcohol and my life has become unmanageable.

2.

What do I do with the time? Where do I go in my head? Who even wants to know me? Why the fuck should they? What's the month after this? Say the alphabet backwards. Say twenty-five Hail Marys and touch your nose with one finger. Wade out in your own self-pity and drown in the sump. Time will kill me.

This guy at Duffy's told us when he first got sober he spent three hours standing in front of a clock saying "one minute at a time." I can't do that. I'm weak.

My mind moves around like worms on a plate. I can look at myself in a mirror and argue with the face, in my head, the face wants me not to open the bottle and has its voice in the back of my head and the voice in the front of my head says open it so that's what I do. That's what I did. That was in the bathroom of a bar called The Gold Clown, dark, with paintings of clowns on black velvet.

Steve isn't dead, Steve is in the mountains. That's what he loves. He takes off by himself and hikes into the mountains. Where did he get that? I saw him in the schoolyard and it broke my heart. He was all alone and I hid behind a tree and saw him by himself. I was by myself. In my head. But I faked it for the outside. Steve did better. That's good. Steve did it better.

If you walk into treatment you must have taken the first

step. I mean if you mean it when you walk in. There are guys go just to get the wife off their backs. Or they get sent from work. Or the court. But if you walk in like me and you can't handle the stairs and you drop your stuff and you're walking dead then you must be taking the first step. Please let me lie down and sleep. Good Christ.

Feeling sorry for myself is sure to get me drunk. Resentment will get me drunk. (Who can I resent? I can fucking resent anyone. No trouble. I could resent the ocean if I tried.) Jeannie loves me she said. She wants to marry me. One born every minute. It's something though, isn't it. Soft legs, belly, lying in a warm bed. I'll make the effort here and clean things up. I'll call Mom and let her know I'm all right. But what? Right, Jeannie's wedding. I stood her up, didn't I? Forget about that.

I can't clean this up. The light is so dim and the smell, I can't take the smell. I'll take a shower and I'll go for a walk and I'll get a meeting book. I'll fill up my life like it's worth something. If I feel sorry for myself I'll get drunk. I am powerless over a fucking chemical. I am a worthless piece of shit but I have some great qualities. I'm sort of unique, you know? My father was a great piano player. He played with Beiderbecke. Pee Wee Russell. Red Nichols. I have a lot of skills. I have a great sense of humor. It's dark in here.

I take a shower and the water is so soft and warm. I could stop here and everything would be all right. There are some clean clothes in the closet. I put them on and I comb my hair and I open the door to the light. At the top of the path it's the four lanes again and the white liquor store in the bright sunlight. I cross the street where the light is and there are lines to walk between.

The Colonial is empty except for Charlie behind the counter. I don't take my eyes off Charlie.

"Hi."

"Jack, Jesus. Good to see you. You look terrific."

No. I look a little better than I did. "Three weeks today."

"You look ten years younger."

"Uh. Yeah. Well I wanted to thank you, Charlie. I mean for putting up with me, the times you gave me food. All that."

"I didn't know what the hell to do. It hurt to look at you, you know?"

"Well, thanks."

"I mean we get bad in here but you were bad. I remember we used to have this guy come in the mornings and one day he was so bad Ernie looks at him through the glass and says, 'He's so fucking hungover he has to jerk off to get his heart started.' That's how you looked, swear to God."

I laugh. I've done that. It's not funny. Someone comes up behind me. I'm in the way so I raise a hand to Charlie and turn around too fast, not casual enough, and bump chests. The guy smirks at me.

"I'll be god-damned. Jack Erdmann. I figured you were dead by now."

I don't even know who he is. Marin County Real Estate for sure. I side-step him.

"You're a real shock, Jack. Scared the hell out of me."

Pissant. Worthless Goddamn Ugly Fucking Parasite Cocksucker.

"Yeah. Well that's how it goes."

I am dead. I'm a shaking corpse. I set out on my walk. Things could be worse. Right. "The sun was shining as Jack walked down the street thinking about everything that had happened that day and all the bright vistas that had suddenly opened to him. He couldn't wait to tell his mother and to give her the check he'd gotten from Mr. Dithers."

Right.

Things move much too fast around me. Things in the corner of my eye like too-big insects fluttering. I look away from people coming toward me. Who knows what they might know? They might know me. Mainly, they all have real lives and it's clear I don't. I should be wearing one of those simple mesh Halloween masks, the ones that used to cost a quarter. A cop car pulls up next to me at the curb. My life has become unmanageable.

"Hey, Jack."

I turn around and look down at the driver.

"Excuse me?"

"Don't remember me, huh?"

I look at him but I don't say anything. Fucking cop. All those years of driving and watching and gulping my heart when I saw the colored lights. The rush of the black/white, blocks away. Hiding in bushes, handcuffs in Reno.

I don't say anything but I half smile. The power smile. The smile in the face of power. He's not my father. He's just another Guy Who Got His Gun.

"We took you to Lincoln House. You look a lot better."

"Oh, geez, yeah, I remember, you know how it is, yeah, I finally got it, you know, been sober three weeks, finally." I'm a buffoon. The cop has the half smirk on his face.

"Yeah, well glad to hear it, Jack." The edge of a threat. Where's the fucking flashlight huh? What the fuck is wrong with me? I'm not a criminal. I turn my back and walk away but I can feel the steps like they're painted out in front of me. Like a high school dance class. Fucking Arthur Murray. Piss on him.

If I were ten years old I'd be stronger. When I was ten years old I was scared but I held it together. I dealt with my father. I dealt with everything. In my bedroom at night the moon would come through the attic windows and brighten the white plaster of my foot high crucifix on the little shiny table, the moon like a spotlight for bad dreams. They gave me the crucifix at school. I was good, I won something. What did I do? Who the fuck knows?

My father's face could fill up any room he was in. You know? My mother was like a substitute world, a soft glade in the tangle. Which is not it. I am a drunk because I am addicted to alcohol because my family is full of drunks all the way back, my father too, and I am addicted so you can take all the horseshit psychology and shove it up your ass, Jack. Yes you can. But God it hurts, it did, all the way back there the bright mornings and the expectations and everything sliding slowly down with no way to stop no way to go but the fake smile.

With or without I'm a drunk, but with I'm an open wound on shoes I don't recognize. Where did I get these shoes?

I don't know, Sister. They must have grown there.

My head is a hollow thing I carry this trapped guy in. I can feel the edges. When I bump myself on the edges I pass out. I slid in the river, I fell on my head, I charmed them in the Reno Looney Bin, I pissed on my life like a wino in a railroad yard. I am a wino in a railroad yard. I need alcohol to stay alive. I think I need alcohol to stay alive. I never would have made it this far. That's the truth. I stop myself in the street and think about it. Could I have made it this far without alcohol? This far? Jesus. Could I have made it to 1968? Probably not, but I really don't know.

More will be revealed.

Jesus, I hope not.

If you curl your body up in a ball and put your arms up so your forearms cover your face and then you stay perfectly still, perfectly nothing, and you don't breathe except in little, shallow, quiet gulps, and you wait and you wait then your balance will come back. That's what I used to think. But it turned out the balance isn't in the mind. It's in your body and when it's gone you can't lie on the floor without holding on. You can curl and rock and hide in the dark but nothing helps.

The dark is full of things. Stuff you never wanted to see. Stuff you forgot that comes back to open you up like a tin can. You know what's frightening? Everything. Every fucking thing is scary when you reach the basement.

The cop car swims ahead down the street like a black fish, a boss fish in the shallows. The sun is out and that's nice. It warms the top of my head.

I know what to do. I stay away from the places I've been and the people I knew. It's like staying away from your life. You feel like you've been written out of the book. Do we need Erdmann? Shit, no, lose him after chapter three.

I've been around, you know? I've been a lot of places. Let's see. I've been in St. Louis, I grew up in St. Louis, and I've been in Oklahoma, and I've been in New York, and I've been in Europe when I was twenty I think, and I've been here, in California, and Nevada, Reno, the Looney Bin, Marin County, the Crisis Center, police stations, dark apartments. And here I am now. I'm taking a walk with my head. It's a rat in a party hat. Happy Birthday Jackie! it says on the hat.

I just want to fit. I want to know how to do these things everybody else is doing. Passing the College of Marin there are all these kids going to school and they sit there and listen because they want to pass so they can get good jobs and be comfortable.

Shit, that isn't true.

But they do pay attention, and they do it, and they lead comfortable lives and raise their kids to be comfortable too.

Boring scumbags. No, that isn't true.

I want to know the things they know and then maybe I won't be scared. I'm scared because I'm all in pieces walking. It's like that pony I was on and my mother dressed me up like a cowboy and sat me on this pony for the photographer.

Out on our street, in the trees. I was all in pieces, made of the pony and the cowboy clothes and the trees and my mom. Where the hell was I? I can't tell from the picture. The pictures are in a big dark book in the nightstand table in the rotten, dark, basement apartment. Take a deep breath.

My father would sit and stare and not know anything. That's later, when I wasn't that much of a kid anymore. They took him to this big, square, dark stone hospital and gave him shock treatments. But he was never really all right. His life was unmanageable. Except for Mom, she had to manage it. The old pictures of Mom are showgirl pictures. She was a dancer. Feather boas and sequins. She was really strong. The men were the weak ones. My father's face is huge and very angry and I want to get away but there's no place to go but my room and he can find me there. In the dark the moonlight on the crucifix. I have stuff on the walls so it looks like a Norman Rockwell kid's room. But underneath, Jesus, underneath is The Basement Apartment and the Long Night.

That's a friend of my son's on the grass, a girl with long, blond hair. The sun is shining. My rat squeaks and takes off his hat. Powerless powerless powerless. What I tell you three times is true. What's that from? I can't remember. I am powerless and my life is unmanageable. Say it as much as I can.

It's very simple. It's like this. It's a bright day and all the other people are here doing things. They do things because that's how the world is. They get by by doing things. Now all I need, I mean really *need*, is food and a place to live. I don't even need a place to live, really. I mean I could sleep on the hillside if I had to. Sure I could. You have to be able to not drink living under a bridge. Uh-huh. But I have the food and the place to live (a black shock here). There are people who still don't mind seeing me, a few. There are meetings. They did it, I'll do it. They're stronger than I am though. No. Wait a minute. It's a bright day and all the other people are here doing things. They aren't afraid. They're lovable. They have that secret quality like the kids with their parents at Forest Park Highlands, my father's arcade, the way they walked around easily together. I was getting the money out of the machines. I'd open them up and the coins went in the box and I'd pull it on a little cart. They were heavy. My father was heavy then too. Got heavier all the time then his face went and he didn't know anything. That's not such a bad thing, not knowing anything. That's not such a bad thing. It's a bright day and the girl with the blond hair crosses in front of me then half bounces across the wide street with her books in front of her in both arms. The sun is out. I will get through this and become a person. I will become semi-conscious but I'll get around and no one will know the difference. That must be the secret. They don't feel their nerves like I feel mine. I'll become a priest and I'll live in a monastery on a hillside and the birds will come to the window. Jesus fucking Christ.

Please help me. I am powerless and my life has become unmanageable. I've got that down anyway. No I don't. We were powerless and our lives had become unmanageable. That's the right way . . .

I have to watch myself every minute. This is no joke.

EIGHTEEN

Just the simple things. Getting up in the morning and brushing my teeth. I do the simple things. I pretty much do what I'm asked to do because others have done it before—they know how and I don't. I'm not used to accepting advice—no drunk is. But they've done it, and I haven't. And they're so bloody kind I could cry.

I'm most afraid that I won't be capable. Colonial Liquors sits in the sunlight every morning, right across the street. I pray raggedly that not too much will be required of me but I know, because of the life I've led, that probably a great deal will be required. I still remember my father's big hands reaching for me but it's not an excuse anymore. He still scares me but it's nothing I can use. His grandfather was an alcoholic and his father was an alcoholic and he was an alcoholic and I'm an alcoholic. *It's a disease.* Sick families are sick families, and if I choose to pretend that I'm an alcoholic because my father was unpredictable and brutal, I'm going to get drunk again. I know this because I've been told. I accept what I've been told because it's all I've got. Accept isn't the same as *feel.* I need to feel it. But I did feel the one thing, I heard the words on the tape and they went down into my solar plexus and eased the muscles. *God could and would if He were sought.* I don't pray to the Catholic God. I pray to the air.

"Hi, Mom."

"How are you, Jack?"

"Good. I'm good, Mom."

"I hope so, Jack. I can't take much more with the phone calls and all."

"I know, Mom. It's okay, it's good."

"How would it be if I came out for Christmas?"

"Well, it's very small here."

"I don't need much, Jack. I'd love to see the children."

"Well, sure."

"Well, I'll get the tickets and you tell them Grandma's coming."

I sit by the phone in the dimness. I clean the refrigerator, the bathroom, and the rest of the kitchen. I take out the garbage. Coming back in I stop in the doorway and study the rest of the room. It has to be done, but first I read the paper. I breathe deeply and evenly. I have to start with my sleeping bag. I'm afraid to, because of the smell. But I do it. I roll it up and put it outside the door. I'll take it to the laundry room later. I sprinkle the pad under it with baking soda. I rub it in then sweep it off. There are old clothes under it. I pick them up gingerly and put them in a laundry bag. One of my socks has a bottle in it, a half pint. I stand there holding it with two fingers. I walk to the garbage that way, and drop it in. My knees are shaking.

I look at the clock. An hour has passed. I open a can of tuna fish and laboriously make a sandwich. I eat it successfully. I wash my hands and sit down in the chair. Now I have to make plans. I look at the clock. Twenty minutes have passed. I call Tom Kay. He's not home so I leave a message on his machine. I call up Tahoe to talk to my kids. There's no answer. I call up Bob at the Lincoln House detox. He's a very nice guy and happy for me. I can hear in his voice that he's not betting on my sobriety, he's worried about it. That depresses me. I jerk my body and head violently, once. How can I be depressed at his doubts. How could any of them not have doubts? I'm a ridiculous man.

I put on a jacket and go out. I walk to the Woodland shopping center and sit in the coffee shop. I drink too much coffee. I can't do anything right. When I start drinking a liquid, I keep drinking. I pick up a couple of mysteries at the College of Marin bookstore. At home I can't read them, they don't make sense. I get through to Tom Kay and he tells me to go out to the garbage can and break the bottle. I do.

The meeting is at 8:30. It's a quarter after seven. I'll walk slow. First I'll take a shower. I'll be *really* clean. When I'm really clean I have to get dressed. It's not too bad except for putting on clean socks. They're tight and bending over makes me dizzy. I open the door when I'm ready and step outside. I walk slowly, but not so slow that it looks like I don't have anywhere to go. There are no Police cars around. I shouldn't care about that. Shouldn't, wouldn't, couldn't. Stick with reality.

The church is in the trees on a dark street. The doorway is bright. I remember the doorway at St. Mary Magdalen's the night of the dance with Joe and the port and the way we felt high and bright. Fuck. It's early so I lean on a tree. That doesn't work so I go inside and read the church announcements on the bulletin board. People are drifting in but no one I know. I'm on my third cup of coffee and I'm shaking. Soon I'll start to sweat. My palms will be sweating by the end of the meeting when we hold hands for the Lord's Prayer. Fuck. I try to plan where I can sit so I can slip out without anyone feeling my hand. I eat half the cookies off the counter.

The speaker is a funny guy. I don't laugh, but I can tell. I'm going to have to learn how to laugh. Jack Erdmann, salesman to the Crowned Heads of Europe, can't laugh at a funny story. I get a couple of phone numbers after the meeting. I walk away by myself, nice and slow.

When I get home, Steve is watching the tube. Here's my big chance.

"Could we talk for a few minutes?"

"Sure."

"I have some amends to make."

"Uh-huh."

"I was a bad father." This is his cue.

"Yeah. Well just take care of your*self*, Dad."

It's not going right.

"Well I need you to know that I love you. No matter how it was, I always loved you."

"Sure. I know."

Goddamn.

"I really need to know how you feel." Shit. I *want* to know how he feels. I don't *need* to, not now. The voices are screwing me up. They told me all about this stuff. They cramp my style.

"I'm happy for you. I hope it works out."

"Oh it'll work out. It's gonna work out."

"Well good."

"Yeah, well thanks for the help."

What am I doing? He looks at me across the room.

"I don't know what you want me to say, Dad."

I put my head in my hands. I'll never be right. What an asshole I am. Steve goes to his girlfriend's place. I go to bed and watch the headlights move on the wall.

Mom gets in three days before Christmas. She's kind enough not to say anything about the crummy apartment. I take her to the supermarket and she buys food and a quart of Gilbey's. The kids come down from Tahoe. It makes me a little bitter. I wonder if they'd have come if Mom wasn't here.

"Knock it off, Jack," my sponsor says.

Mom drinks every day about five. It's hard to watch. She has two and things begin to tumble out of her. St. Louis and George and what a good boy I was. What Dad said to her on the way to the hospital.

"It made everything all right. As soon as he said that he said 'I've always needed you, haven't I, Marian?' I knew it was all worth it."

She's sixty-five and discovering the cocktail hour. I stay away from the bottle. I can't handle the smell.

"It used to kill me when he hit you, Jack, but he thought he was doing the right thing and . . . "

I guess he did. I guess he tried to. I tried to. I always tried to think I was doing the right thing. Most people do. That's what doing the best you can means.

". . . he *always* loved you and I hope you never forget that."

I won't forget, Mom. I don't *know* it though. It's something I'd like to know, but I don't. I won't.

"We all do the best we can and we didn't know about pills in those days. How could we? He did stop drinking though, it's just we didn't know about the pills."

I remember her hand on the back of my head. I'm up in her arms, crying, and she's holding me up with just one arm and the other hand on the back of my head. These are the feelings that count. These are the feelings I'm afraid of. How did that happen? How did I get scared of the only feelings that meant anything?

I made myself up wrong. I made up the wrong person. I didn't know. I drank so I'd never know. The alcohol didn't want me to know.

Marian sits in the light from the television finishing her second martini. A tough, marvelous, church-ridden Irish woman. She cooks in our little kitchen, cheerfully. She swirls her skirt and does a little dance step.

"Now we're going to Midnight Mass for Christmas Eve and that's the end of it. I haven't missed one in twenty years and I'm not going to start now."

Christmas is hard. All those old feelings. The season creeping up with the colors. Snow in St. Louis. The expectations. Maybe everything will be all right, it's Christmas. Just for one day, please. When it isn't all right, the kids blame themselves. Looking at Christmas trees.

But off we go. It's terrific. Father Tuohy is drunk in the parking lot. He's directing traffic into a cul-de-sac. "Goddamn you," he yells, "learn how to drive." No snow in California. I'd wake up in my room and when it had snowed in the night it was like the world had been lifted into a higher, cleaner air. Our sleds on the hillsides. "Will you do what I goddamn tell you to do. Will you do that?" the priest yells.

Well, hell, he's drunk. I know that pain.

Bridget and Dave are in Tahoe with Sara. Steve is here. Steve and Mom get along well. He teases her, and she likes that. She blossoms.

"Jack used to get so angry at me when I'd dance. He was just a little thing then and he'd get all red and angry when I danced. You remember that, Jack. Virginia and I used to laugh and laugh."

"You must have laughed when I wasn't there."

"Oh of course we did. You were such a serious little boy. We'd never laugh in front of you."

Steve smiles. A serious little boy at lit-up Christmas. Down the line—one serious little boy to another like strung decorations on the one big tree.

It would be nice if the outside were snowy, like it used

to be. We had snow in Tahoe. (DON'T THINK ABOUT THAT.) The kids were still pretty young. There were the Christmases in Mill Valley. We went fishing. (DON'T FUCKING THINK ABOUT THAT.) Mom is lost in thought. She rouses herself.

"You even had that dream once, Jack, remember. He had this dream that we were standing by his bed and laughing at him. So long ago." She sips her drink. "It was so long ago."

Not really. There isn't any piece of pain or embarrassment I don't have at my fingertips. It was yesterday. It happened this morning.

"I thought he might be a priest he was such a serious little boy. And you prayed so beautifully. He helped his father pray too. Did you know that, Steve? He used to sit with his father when the sickness started and help him to pray."

I did, didn't I? Did it help? I guess it helped. It helped him.

"Remember the church in Tahoe?" Steve says. I shake my head at him.

"Yes?" Mom says.

"Oh, nothing. Dad just had an argument with the priest was all."

"That's not like you, Jackie."

"No, Mom. I wasn't feeling well."

We have a little Christmas tree that Marian bought. It isn't much, but in the quiet light it has a nice glow to it. Like everything else. Sometimes it's fine and sometimes it opens on all the fear in the world. When I'm not RIGHT HERE, right in the present, every goddamn thing opens on something else and pretty soon I'm streaming away into the past or the future. They both suck.

Bob at Lincoln House told me "You've got one foot in the past and one foot in the future, Jack. You know what that means?"

"Uh, yeah. No. I don't know."

"Means you're pissing on the present."

Steve says, "It wasn't a bad argument or anything, just kind of funny for Christmas."

I glare at him but I can't bring it off.

"Remember how you served the Mass, Jackie, back home? What was that friend of yours' name, Harry, with the bright cheeks, Harry something? The two of them were up there every Sunday just so sweet and serious."

I smile. It's a slow smile and it feels good on my face. "We were drunk, Mom."

"No no, Jack, I mean way back when you were an altar boy, you and Harry."

"We were drunk."

Mom looks at me. "Now how could you have been drunk then?"

"We drank the wine in the Sacristy. Every week."

I can't stop smiling.

"Serious business," Steve says.

"Oh, Jack."

"I'm confessin', Mom."

"And that nice Harry boy?"

"That's right."

"Well, I guess you never know."

I start to laugh. Steve laughs too. It's magic and just for the second (a second is everything—time isn't the same where I am), the world is like a snowy flower.

Nothing makes any sense. We're sitting in this long narrow, street-level apartment at Christmas time. I'm scared, Steve is who knows? Mom is drunk, and it feels pretty good, RIGHT NOW it feels pretty good. There's a real thread of affection here—of blood, love, memory. Where did it come from? It came from nowhere.

I think of all of us happy with each other, and relaxed. It

isn't possible and I can't find a single coherent reason why it should be possible. The weight of the past is too much. It is. It must be.

The streetlights shine on the windows and there's just enough of a chill in the air so you might think of winter in St. Louis. An impossibly mild winter. How many years can you fit in an instant? I'm following my father's big footsteps over the broken ground again. I'm the same person, I'm just bigger. That's where the soul is, I think, in the way of seeing that's always the same and the voice in the back of the head.

Mom is talking. The light from the floor lamp reflects yellow off Steve's glasses.

"We had some good times, didn't we, Jack? It wasn't all the way it got. Remember how you loved the Arcade? And when you'd sit under the piano when George played? He'd hold on to the big piano leg like he might blow away."

In the soft light she looks young and beautiful again. It's not just the light. It's me. I'm not pretending, either. And I'm not fucking drunk. And I'm not sentimental and I see my life for what it was. For all of us. And I'm not a fool. And I'm not filled with peace and gladness and I wish to hell things had been different and I could have lived a different life. For all of us.

And I'm not confident. I'm a drink away from Hell's terminal. And I'm not strong. And I'm not courageous. And I'm not planning for the future, like a real person.

"We never stopped loving each other, did we, Jackie? That's the important thing."

My eyes fill up with tears so I get up and go to the refrigerator.

"Nobody's perfect. You just have to do the best you can."

"That's about it," Steve says.

I can't stop crying. I'm standing in front of the open refrigerator down at the dark end of the room. I don't know if they can hear me. I'd rather they didn't, but that makes me feel dishonest, not a good way for me to feel. "At least you know it," I think.

"Should I make you something to eat, Jack?"

"No, Mom. I'll be right there."

At the other end of the room Mom and Steve are talking comfortably. I dry my eyes with a dishtowel. I'm out of the machinery and nothing will ever be that bad again. It couldn't be.

Because I'm out and I don't have to use my own strength to stay out. I have faith. It astounds me.

"Are you sure, Jack? Are you sure you're not hungry?"

"Take it easy, Mom. I'm okay."

I'm not of course. But in the dark at the end of the room in the light from the refrigerator, I'm not scared. Not for the instant. I'm a middle aged man with hope. I'm a person, not an object, and I won't drink anymore or be a slave anymore, and I won't see that look in Steve's eyes anymore and I won't terrify that poor woman and I will, I will think of myself as a decent person with substance and patience and grace and Jesus, I almost smile. I haven't stopped shaking yet, not completely. I can't think like this. I'm nowhere. I've just gotten started, I'm nowhere. I need to move slowly and tomorrow I'm setting up the chairs at the church. I won't set them up better or worse than anyone else. I'll just set them up. I smile and close the door. As it closes I know I've been staring at Marian's bottle.

All the help in the world. I have all the help in the world and all the help out of the world. The door clicks. I turn around and I see the back of Steve's head fuzzed in the light. His head was little once, Mom's too. My head, and George's head and Arthur's and Louis Karl's. Little, expectant heads all in a row. We didn't expect much, not really. To be loved.

To not be panicked. I can't make *it* different. But if *I'm* different, well, we can see what happens.

Whatever it is, it won't be worse. I goddamn well *know* that. Something I know. I *know* something. I want to tell them, like a kid.

The thing is, see, I tell myself walking back, the thing is I have all the time, and all the help in the world. I'm not alone at all, and maybe I can touch other people as I've been touched. With grace, maybe.

That's what I hope for and that's what I need, walking, gingerly, halfway down the room toward people I love and can *see* without fear. Maybe my life can move like it's supposed to, like a growing thing with no wheels, no rails, and no dark terminal. Maybe like a vine does, turning with the light.

My hands are dangling helplessly, but they feel okay, and it's suddenly clear that something I've been told is true— that God knows more about me than I know about myself. What a relief.

There isn't any end to that room—one end opens on my floating, praying corpse and the other on stories and stories and more stories, nightmares and epiphanies and the sheer laboriousness of coming back to life.

Coming back to life is no fun. It's hard, and your nerves make a noise like a rusted-out engine trying to turn over.

It's a job you have to do. Not because you're getting paid, not because you want to look good, not because you'll get your wife back—not because you'll get anything back. Maybe you will and maybe you won't.

You do it because there are others, and when you ask for help it's there. So that in at least one part of your life you're not a kid anymore, looking for answers with no one to ask.

I've never had another drink, and in my life now I try to give some time to a proposition that I've come to believe covers all of human obligation—we need to pass on less pain than we receive.

Knowing at the end of the story, with the light fading, that none of it was for nothing and that through all the pain you managed, finally, to pass on less than you got.

It's how the volume of human misery can decrease, and how sobriety works.

EPILOGUE

I needed to write this book because sobriety maintains itself by helping others get sober. So if you're an alcoholic, or live in an alcoholic family, I wrote it for you.

If you've read it, you're alive—it doesn't matter how bad things are or what you've lost or what you think you've lost. The fact is you're still alive and things can change. That's something to hold on to.

If you recognized yourself in the book, then you can begin to understand that you're more like other human beings than unlike them, and that you're surrounded by men and women who share your experience and would love to help pull you out of the machinery.

There are plenty of theoretical books on alcoholism. It's strange—they aren't much help, but there they are. There isn't much of a market for theoretical books on diabetes—a book for diabetics that recommends will power and high sugar intake probably won't sell. The market for theoretical books on construction is small. A man who speculates in print that the best way to build a house is from the top down probably won't make it big.

But the alcoholic is open game for everyone. It seems that any reasonably coherent combination of personal resentment, moral one-upmanship and bogus statistics will get an author by.

So I felt I had to do something apart, and everything I knew about alcoholism told me that good intentions aren't enough, that you can't reach a drunk with a well-meaning tract.

You can't scare a drunk either, not for long, and if you appeal to his reason you're only appealing to the part of him that rationalizes. So I thought I'd write a book that would do what the alcoholic would rather not have done—touch him in those places where he can't bear to be touched, the emotional places where he remembers who he was and who he wanted to be.

When you drink alcoholically, the memories that hurt most won't be the memories of pain but the memories of the times when it seemed that things might be all right. It's a clue to the alcoholic reality. The good memories will eventually hurt the most.

You're doing what you can to kill the pain but the worst pain is attached to things that didn't even hurt. It's simple— you know how things really are, and you can't look. You know they could have been different, and that hurts worse than anything. When the memory involves a parent whose love was blocked by alcohol too, the pain is violent.

"Sooner or later the world will break your heart," the Irish saying goes. Well if you're a practicing alcoholic your heart is already broken. And the world didn't do it, the alcohol did. This is the secret of alcohol. The alcohol creates the symptoms you think it's treating.

It's even worse than that. Whatever you are most afraid

of, that's what the alcohol will finally create. It doesn't seem at all that way when you start. When I started, the alcohol told me there was a way out, that the pain could be killed.

Then it told me to kill the pain at all costs.

I don't want anyone to think that this was the story of a child abused by a family—it wasn't—it was the story of a family abused by alcohol. My family had the one, minimal chance that George might wake up one morning and decide to get out of the machinery. But his emotions ruled that out.

When you wake up in a house where alcohol has taken over, when you live in one, every corner is linked to every other by fine threads of fear. No one wants to talk about anything—last night, last week, last year—because the fear of the unpredictable has become worse than the reality of the misery. Maybe it'll be a good day, maybe nothing will happen today, maybe life will be different, starting right now.

The interesting thing is that at the center of all this is a drunk who frequently wakes up thinking exactly the same things. So where do you go? No one wants things to be the way they are, but no one can change it but the drunk. And he thinks with two heads. The stronger head is the one where the alcohol lives.

It hurts a lot when a kid thinks it's his fault that a parent doesn't love him. The pain is not bearable. So there are adaptations to make, and attitudes to strike. "I can just look out the window and I won't care. If I step on every line from here to the corner, he won't be home when I get back. If nobody knows I care then they can't laugh at me. If I don't say anything then they won't tell me it's my fault and I have to go away. If I don't get scared right away I can think of something to do. Don't do anything right away. Think of what to do."

From one generation of alcoholic family to the next, the figure of the deeply confused and frightened child is pretty much a constant. The child has no frame of reference. He doesn't know how things are supposed to be, he only knows how things are. Then he begins to notice the outside and it tells him things like "Parents love their children." He can tell that something is wrong. Well, whose fault is that?

In the alcoholic family, children have to make themselves up out of speculation, fear and occasional panic. The misery is everywhere. We pass it from generation to generation like a family Christmas stocking with a snake in it.

A drunk falls into a Christmas tree in slow motion. The last thing he wants to do, the last thing he'd ever have thought of doing. A child watches and twists around in his head. "Please don't do that, you don't have to do that, don't let Mommy scream, please stop it!"

Alcoholism is not an emotional disorder, but it does have emotional triggers. I suppose one could be born with a genetic predisposition to alcoholism and never have the disease develop, but in this society it's not bloody likely.

For anyone born with the disposition, whose life provides the triggers, there isn't much hope. Because that first drink will open him up like a flower, physically and emotionally, and he'll keep coming back for more.

The fact is alcohol is a chemical and its effects are cold, mechanical, and predictable. When you begin drinking alcoholically, you get on a train. You neither grow nor learn emotionally, you just ride. The last station is hell. And when you get there, you remember you left behind tickets for your children.

The next time you walk in the street, look for the faces of kids with their parents. You can tell which ones are in pain. You only have to look. Try to see them figuring. They have a code to break and they think all the time.

The sadness is overwhelming. A child who has figured out

that he is not acceptable to the people who are supposed to love him has to become someone else. He has to learn how to stand, and talk, and smile. He has to have a way to indicate that he doesn't care what anybody thinks. But he can't ever say that, or be obvious about it. He needs to be able not to cry. He needs to talk to God too, but he can't let anyone know about that. Talking to God is weak and crazy.

I started to drink alcoholically in Church, when I drank the wine. It was a communion.—I was joined to alcohol by a bond deeper than any other. It was also, like a child's first communion, a formality. I was alcoholic already, I was born that way.

When I say I was born alcoholic I mean that I had a genetic predisposition to become addicted to alcohol. There are people who want to argue about this. I don't have the energy.

Ask any recovering alcoholic how his first drink made him feel. Then ask a non-alcoholic. Compare. Try the academic approach. Take twenty randomly selected volunteers and gradually, with measured doses, physically addict them to alcohol. Cut them off cold turkey, let them go through being sick, then tell them the experiment was flawed and it has to be done again. Notice that most walk away while some ask "When do we start?"

Here's the absolute center of the horror—the predisposition to alcoholism responds strongly to emotional triggers which overwhelmingly tend to be present in families with alcoholic histories. Alcohol creates in families, much as it physically does in individual bodies, the conditions necessary to its power.

To an early adolescent whose family has been a swirling mystery of tenderness, inexplicable violence, and day-to-day apprehension, alcohol is sublime. It opens out, just as the world is beginning to, on dreams of sex and power. To the same adolescent who is already predisposed to alcoholism, alcohol is salvation.

When the alcoholic starts to drink, the world becomes a brand new place. You go out on the street early and it's like a bright movie-set. It's your goddamn world, with flowers growing in front yards. You feel like you belong—you're a logical part of everything. You feel whole.

If you recognize these feelings, I put it to you that this is not at all how non-alcoholics feel after their first drunks.

Alcohol will let you do a lot of things. Most of all, it simplifies your responses. You need to celebrate? Have a drink. You need to grieve? Have a drink. You're nervous, you're sad, you're bored, you're resentful? Have a drink.

You want revenge? You want to make the people who care about you suffer? You really want to let them know how you feel? Fuck 'em. Hold the glass up to the light and knock it back.

When the machinery gets going, it's quiet and smooth. You can hardly hear it. You're born in the station, you get yourself a ticket, you get on the train. It's a good-looking crowd, too. All your friends are there. A lot of your friends, anyway. You're not going to have too many friends who leave drinks at the bar to go home. You put up your feet and strike a pose. You have a million of 'em.

People come to see you and you chat. You go to other compartments. Train compartments are secret and sexual— the low rumble from the tracks, the feeling of being between places. You've got what you need and it wasn't that hard.

There are a few things to take care of but they're all just forms, really, families and stuff like that. You have to get close to somebody then fence off your compartment. Life is a journey, isn't it? No shit.

When you get sick, take it like a man. We all do at the bar. A little humor, a couple of drinks. Pay the bills. It's nobody's goddamn business how you feel. There are things that have to be done. Real things. Take care of the feelings and do what has to be done. It's a kind of dignity.

Everything is open and you're moving. You know the woman two compartments up? She has a mouth like a flower. Think about her and look out the window. It's a solid, smooth ride. The way the frost gets on the side of the glass, the first taste, the cold gin in the sunlight. You're in here and they're out there and that's the way to get along.

Along and along and along. The saddest, mechanical monologue. What goes on when you talk to yourself on a moving train? Not much. The important thing that happens is you move farther down the track.

There's arrogance when you're young and you can hold your liquor and you're getting laid and you can move through the official world secretly, laughing and cutting corners. It's a bright life, and you're one of the chosen. If someone had said to me "Jack, you're an alcoholic," I would have said "Yeah. What about it?"

The romance of alcohol, the aura of alcohol, the literate and sexual connotations, the allowances made, the humor, the bravery, the camaraderie, the power, the glory, the tragic weakness.

Alcohol is a full life. There are accommodations to be made so it looks right, so you're not just crouched under a trestle with a paper bag. (Which you could be, much more easily than you think. All it takes is a slight adjustment in your ability to pay.)

When you sit in a group in a recovery house and listen to the stories, you quickly discover that the vile sins the alcoholic thinks he's been guilty of are largely the sad and frightened sins of the child who's trying to think his way out of his life. It'll take a week of work for a drunk to get up the courage to tell a room full of other drunks that he used to wish his father were dead.

He has no frame of reference. He's lived alone in his head for so long that he really doesn't know that other people think these things. Or maybe he does know it, he just doesn't feel it. The confusion is so deep it feels like the room is full of extremely articulate six year olds.

(Which is not a bad feeling at all. If you've been in a recovery house group you can say that you've been in a room-ful of people all of whom were trying to tell the truth. When was the last time you could say that?)

In the recovery house groups the businessmen start their stories in terms of who they were in the community, how much they made, what beautiful children they have. The other drunks just sit there and wait. There's very little bullshit that can survive a roomful of drunks trying to be honest. When the bullshit does survive, it's fatal.

"Well, I just had my business really off the ground and the pressures got to me. I don't know if you know what it's like trying to keep it together in times like these but it's rough, you better believe that."

But, sadly, nobody does.

"Tell you the truth my wife and I haven't been getting along all that well. That has something to do with it. And I worry about the kids. I'd do anything for the kids."

No response. Everyone knows the flat truth. As far as the alcoholic's social persona goes, he doesn't have relationships, he takes hostages. It doesn't matter how much he wanted a family or how much he loves his kids.

The addictive urge is primary and automatic, and in the half light that descends when you want a drink but know you shouldn't have one, "Fuck 'em," is what you hear. It uses other words when it needs to, but way down the line, where the alcohol doesn't have to pretend anymore, "Fuck 'em," is what it says. It only takes a second, just long enough for the first drink.

The nasty truth is that when a practicing alcoholic creates a family he creates a support system for his alcoholism. His family's fear will make them minimize, cover for him, and cry by themselves. Because the fear of collapse is usually worse than the dull, day-to-day misery.

This is pretty much the edge of hell.

When you get near the end of the line you find out that every drink you took helped compress the fear as if it were a huge spring in your chest. When the alcohol stops working it lets the spring go and suddenly there's nothing in your life but sickness and time and the pain of the past.

Alcohol starts out strong and gets stronger. Whatever it needs to say, it will say. In the late stages, the terminal stages, the mental characteristics of alcoholism are virtually indistinguishable from paranoid schizophrenia. It isn't surprising.

The addiction is primary and it argues with you. There's a second voice in your head, wheedling and raging. And it physically attacks the sheathing around your nerves. Then there's the fact that as you sink you become more visible to others. No matter how you're dressed or where you are, you're unsightly—you know it. People are looking at you.

You're quite mad. It doesn't matter what you really need, what you'll act on is the need for alcohol. And if you see yourself clearly and know you have to stop, the other voice will tell you what it always tells you—kill the pain at all cost. Then you pass into the other world where unreal things are real, and you see them. You always knew you had to stop— this is not where you wanted to be. And you still know you have to stop. But now it's hell.

Everything is gone and there's nothing in the world that doesn't hurt. You aren't going anywhere. You have no balance. You have to be careful not to move your eyes too fast. Your nerves shriek when they don't have alcohol.

All you have now is strength. It's an incredible strength. Years of hangovers and years of faking it and years of turning your mind away from what you don't want to see—they've all added up to an incredible, utterly perverse strength. You can say to yourself "I'm still alive, something may happen." You can cross a room slowly and have to say that before each step.

You still haven't reached the worst, though. If you think it's the worst, you underestimate your capacity for pain.

I get nervous when I hear people say they'll never drink again because they nearly died the last time, or because they remember how bad everything felt. First of all because nobody can really remember pain. Second, because when you're really, finally arrived at your last-stop drunkenness, you're not afraid of dying.

Dying isn't that scary and if you could get it together enough to die, well, that might be great. What you'd really like is to have something do it for you.

You'll wake up in the morning and look in the mirror hopefully for a sign of the Fatal Disease. You already have a fatal disease but it's too fucking painful—you need something else that'll let you go to bed and die with a drink in your hand.

So the idea of staying sober because alcohol will kill you is unreliable at best. You don't stay sober because you're scared of dying. Everybody dies. And you don't stay sober because you understand about alcoholism.

Here it is. I know a drunk who woke up under a sheet in the Morgue. He sat up and looked around at the other white sheets in the dark. He had a tag on his toe. He got out of there and got a drink.

★ ★ ★

I need to say this again, as clearly as possible: The facts of my life did not make me an alcoholic. They didn't make me any crazier, or any more in pain, than any other drunk who's come the same distance down the line.

If you're alcoholic, and you live long enough, this is where you're going. It's a place. It's a goddamn empty train station where it's cold and the sun is just going down.

You are not dealing with a painful reality, you are not a romantic isolato, you are not a secret judge. You are a certified addict to the public view. No one else comes near the station, but it's not like they can't see you. You are addicted to a chemical and it is right on the edge of taking you away completely. It would be better if it did, because the pain is not to be borne. What's happening to your soul is not describable.

My story doesn't say that if you have a brutal, alcoholic father, this is how you'll end up. And it doesn't say that if you're secret and sensitive this is how you'll end up.

It says that if you are an alcoholic, and you drink, this is your last stop. And that when you get here you're going to want to die because of the pain and the fear and the certainty of what you've done to the people who cared for you. You may or may not be able to get it together enough to die.

I once heard a drunk say, "I wanted to save my ass but I found out it was attached to my soul." Exactly. When I was writing about arriving at Duffy's and I typed "One of them shakes as he tries to get the suitcase latched," I started to cry—those who have nothing share the only substance they can find.

When you're lucky enough to come back, you find your life rooted in paradox. There are people who can't handle that. It irritates them, deep down. They write books to prove that it can't work. "Alcoholism is not a disease, it's a very bad habit," they'll tell you.

All I need to know about the matter is that on one side we have a ragtag collection of PhDs, psychiatrists, and resentful moralists all laying claim to insights into the alcoholic condition. On the other side we have millions of recovering alcoholics.

I leave it for you to decide which offers the reliable information.

Anyone who is troubled by the absence of theory can look at it this way. The pre-Newtonians may have lacked an adequate theory of gravitation, but they damn well knew about stepping off cliffs.

"The worst day I've had sober is better than the best day I had drunk." Is that true? Well, it is and it isn't. In the deepest sense, it's perfectly true. The best day I had as a drunk never even happened—it was a fantasy.

"An alcoholic is an egomaniac with an inferiority complex." Is that true? Entirely. Does it make sense? It makes perfect sense to an egomaniac with an inferiority complex.

"You gain strength when you give up." Yes, you do. You see yourself accurately in the universe. You find out how helpless you are, ask for strength, and get it. When you wake up in the morning and know that you are more like other people than unlike them, you're stronger.

"If you throw away what you thought you knew, the bullshit will stay thrown away and the real stuff will come back." You find out the problem isn't over-intellectualization or rationalizing or unbreakable mental pattern. Those are symptoms. The problem is the toxic mind. The fact is, your best thinking got you where you are. So knock it off for a while.

"If you want to keep it, you have to give it away." This

is precisely how it works and how everything should work. This is grace made visible.

When the past comes back now, it comes back in waves. Sometimes for several days at a time. I've been sober now for almost twenty years, but it still hurts.

I'll be sitting in my chair with the sun outside in the trees, feeling fine, like I have a place, and it's real, and suddenly there'll be a slice in my chest, as if I've been cut with a razor. And right behind the cut is a wet past full of hurt faces and murderous bric-a-brac. Little things—minor embarrassments and petty cruelties.

They feel like they could kill. When the hollow, floating feeling comes back, I'm just a scared kid again.

I don't drink, though. What To Do With The Pain is one of the things I've had to learn. If I hadn't I would have ended up back in the dark of the bar with my face in the mirror like a fish in a tank.

And that's just the romance of it. Where I really would have ended up is scrabbling at hard ground with my fingernails, crying for a drink.

What to do with the pain? The fact is it's just like everyone else's pain. I am more like other human beings than I am unlike them. So it isn't even a real question anymore.

What I do with the pain is sit in my chair and feel it. When I do, I'm outside the machinery—the mechanics of alcohol have no access to me.

The drunk is not only dying and killing, he's tending to the volume of human misery—passing on his measured portions to terrified kids who take it in, kill the pain to get along, then pass it on to their own bewildered, frightened children.

I have a painting on my wall of Louis Karl Erdmann, my great grandfather. He looks bland. His eyes are blue and blank. He's wearing a black, frock coat and he has a medal for good marksmanship on his lapel. He looks bland and substantial. I can't see his demons.

I don't really have to, I know them well enough. He died in delirium tremens when he was fifty-six. He left two sons, Emil and Arthur. Emil died young. When he was broke he traded Louis Karl's matched revolvers for a bottle of rye.

Arthur, my grandfather, made his liquor in his basement. He seemed to be a soft, frightened man. Together with Martha, who was strong, he made George, my father. George got Arthur's softness and Martha's arrogance. He also got alcoholism.

His panic didn't seem to be attached to anything. It seemed pure, like a distillation of all the childhood fears of God knows how many alcoholic generations. He passed it on to me.

And I didn't know anything until I saw the guy with the shaking hands helping the fallen drunk on Duffy's stairs.

The compassion of the helpless comes from nowhere. It comes out of the heart of things, and it opens the world.

So I pray, and I meet with other alcoholics, and I try to pass along what I have. I stay sober. In a roomful of men and women trying as hard as they can, common humanity becomes a substance and Grace is in the air.

The simplest bits of kindness make prayers. There's nothing else like it, nothing I know of.

When the pain comes back, I let it hurt. And each time it's a little weaker. It's all simple. Not easy, perhaps, but simple. What you do is you ask for help. Just for the day. "Please help me not to drink today."

Anybody can stay sober for 24 hours, especially if he has other sober drunks to help him. If you want to drink tomorrow, you can drink tomorrow. When you make it through the day, you say thank you. When you wake up, you ask for help. If you decide you don't like what you've got, your misery is refundable. If anyone wants to know where the information came from he can be directed to a miles-high pile of corpses.

I haven't had a drink in twenty years. All I have is gratitude and faith. I'm not one of those drunks who tells you that now he has a beautiful wife, an expensive home and a fat bank account. Those things are utterly irrelevant to sobriety, and to what keeps you sober.

Gratitude spins in the back of my head like a kid's gyroscope. At meetings I sometimes hear speakers whose lives are marvelous, and perfect, and filled with all the things they want. I believe them, it works that way for some. It doesn't matter much to me though whether or not I get the things I want. I've had a lot of trouble with the things I've wanted. Now I've got what I need.

I need my kids and I have them. Their easy presence is a miracle. I could sit down with Bridget and say "You are my sunshine," in a slow, serious voice and there wouldn't be any trace in it of either parody or self-consciousness.

Dave and Steve have an easy and delicate way with me that stays in the present but leaves the past open.

In one of my old magazines there's a wartime Bill Mauldin cartoon. Two GI's are crouched in a foxhole and the air is full of tracer bullets. One of them is saying "I feel like a fugitive from the Law of Averages." Exactly.

There are times when I'm completely filled with a sense of where I am and how I got here, and when I am there's a peace I can't describe except to say that no pain can touch it. When it happens I know everything was worth it, that nothing can ever take it away from me, and that I need to give it away as best I can.

★   ★   ★

So I wrote this to explain. Not to explain myself. That has an edge of apology to it and I don't want to apologize. I wish I'd lived differently, but I didn't.

What I want to explain is that if you're alcoholic, or you live with an alcoholic, things don't have to be the way they are. I want you to believe me because you understand I have no reason to lie to you.

I can see the pain in the faces of people I know, people with houses, and professional veneers, and things. I can see it in the faces of the poor and their children—the drunk I saw with his child in a pushcart on the Embarcadero, both of them trying to understand.

It's always the same—the same goddamn pain romanticized, and trivialized, and dully accepted. It wires families together for generations, the children learning to keep their shoulders tense against the random shocks. They think it must be their fault.

And then *they* raise children who have tense shoulders and chests full of jangling fear and grief.

None of it's necessary. It's time to stop.

ABOUT THE AUTHORS

A former salesman, Jack Erdmann is now an author and lecturer in San Francisco. He has been sober for twenty years.

Larry Kearney is a poet and novelist. He was born in Brooklyn in 1943, moved to San Francisco in 1964, and subsequently published nine books of poetry. He was drunk between 1959 and 1981 but hasn't been since.